THE HISTORY OF RAP MUSIC

AFRICAN-AMERICAN ACHIEVERS

THE HISTORY OF RAP MUSIC

Cookie Lommel

CHELSEA HOUSE PUBLISHERS
Philadelphia

Chelsea House Publishers
Editor in Chief Sally Cheney
Production Manager Pamela Loos
Picture Editor Judy Hasday
Art Director Sara Davis
Managing Editor James D. Gallagher
Senior Production Editor J. Christopher Higgins

Staff for THE HISTORY OF RAP MUSIC
Editorial Assistant Brian Baughan
Associate Art Director Takeshi Takahashi
Designer Keith Trego
Picture Researcher Marty Levick
Cover Design Keith Trego

7 9 8 6

The Chelsea House World Wide Web address is
http://www.chelseahouse.com

Library of Congress Cataloging-in-Publication Data

Lommel, Cookie.
The history of rap music / by Cookie Lommel.
  p. cm. — (African-American achievers)
Includes bibliographical references and index.
Summary: Traces the development of rap music from origins
in the hip-hop of the 1970s through various controversies to
its widespread popularity in the 1990s.
ISBN 0-7910-5820-4 — ISBN 0-7910-5821-2 (pbk.)
1. Rap (Music)—History and criticism. [1.Rap (Music)]
I. Title. II. Series.
ML3531.L66 2000
782.421649'09 — dc21   00-022274

*Frontispiece: Many rap artists have
become known for their flashy styles,
as seen in this picture of 1980s star
Slick Rick, who is sporting several
pounds of gold jewelry.*

CONTENTS

AFRICAN-AMERICAN ACHIEVERS

THE HISTORY OF RAP MUSIC

1

The Language of Music

THE SOUTHERN CALIFORNIA night glittered with stars on February 24, 1999, but none shone so brightly as the young and lovely hip-hop chanteuse Lauryn Hill. Nominated for no less than ten Grammy Awards, a high honor for any singer or musician, Hill carried home five, a record for a female artist. The former member of the Fugees received the Grammy for Best New Artist, and her album, *The Miseducation of Lauryn Hill*, won awards for both Best R&B Album and Album of the Year. Her single "Doo Wop (That Thing)" grabbed top honors as Best R&B Song and Best Female R&B Vocal Performance. Magazines across America trumpeted her success as evidence that 1999 was the Year of the Woman in music; the 41st Grammys had overwhelmingly rewarded female performances, with awards going to Hill's fellow female vocalists Shania Twain, Madonna, Sheryl Crow, Celine Dion, and Brandy, among others.

But amid the hoopla surrounding music's Year of the Woman, another milestone in American and global music was reached in 1999. It was also the 21st year of rap music. Lauryn Hill, a young African American who was a highly visible example of a

In 1999 hip-hop star Lauryn Hill, a former member of the Fugees, won five Grammy Awards. Along with setting a record for a female artist, Hill's achievement proved the ever-growing influence of rap in American music.

rapper who sprang from hip-hop culture, had just dominated the nation's premiere music event. With penetrating lyrics and vocal precision, Hill's lyrics combined a mixture of soul-searching, family importance, and spiritual salvation. Her success showed that a rap artist could walk the fine line between impressing mainstream critics and satisfying hard-core hip-hop fans. The 41st Grammy Awards proved that rap was not a trend that would exhaust itself and burn away, forgotten by all but the urban black community that had invented its powerful voice. Instead, rap—led by superstars like Lauryn Hill and Will Smith, who at the 41st Grammys won Best Rap Solo Performer for the second time— had crossed over into the nation's mainstream.

Of course, rap has always been in much of the nation's bloodstream, carried to the shores of America in the veins of Africans forced into slavery. Rap springs from the same African roots that brought America its many distinctive musical forms, such as ragtime, jazz, blues, and rock 'n' roll. For many reasons Americans have failed to understand the historical roots of rap music and the highly traditional African culture from which hip-hop draws its strengths. As writer Gary O. Clement recognized in a 1993 article in *Upscale* magazine, "Rappers today are keeping alive the oral tradition in our music."

Rappers have been compared to the storytellers of African culture, called griots. Their functions were important and varied. Griots sang songs of praise, of both men and gods. They could alter or maintain the status of individuals or groups. They remembered and recited laws and genealogies, keeping safe all of the knowledge of their orally based culture. They entertained their audiences, and they educated their people. They admonished the bad to be good and urged the good to be better. They required and inspired the participation of their people in events and, by extension, in com-

munities. And they taunted their enemies, pushed them to fear, and communicated messages of war and resistance.

The structure of griot storytelling—chanted rhymes punctuated by the rhythm of drums—underlies modern rap music, as it does so much of 20th-century black poetry and musical expression, such as R&B. This structure forms the foundation of black verbal communication as well; everything from toasts to insults for enemies follows the basic drumbeats and rhymes of the ancient and revered griot tradition. Rap follows and, with newly arranged urban themes and sounds, extends a distinctly African form of communication that even generations of slavery could not destroy. Rap is the new thread connecting the young to the old, the disenfranchised to the warrior, the broken family unit to

In this photograph taken in 1862, African-American slaves work in the fields of a Southern plantation. Like the blues and jazz, rap music has its roots in the culture that African slaves brought to America. Many observe parallels between rap music and the songs of griots, African entertainers and storytellers.

A flyer for a minstrel show in Louisiana. Although for the most part African Americans were treated as second-class citizens even in the years after emancipation, black entertainers appealed to people of all races.

a powerful African community. Rap is the sum of the history of the African experience in 20th-century America. The experience is often disturbing, but it shakes with a dawning sense of power.

Rap arose from a segregated and deprived community. In her book *Black Noise: Rap Music and Black Culture in Contemporary America*, Tricia Rose, a professor of history and African studies at New York University, defines rap music. She describes it as "a form of rhymed storytelling accompanied by highly rhythmic, electronically based music. It began in the mid-1970s in the South Bronx in New York City as a part of hip-hop, an African-American and Afro-Caribbean youth culture composed of graffiti, breakdancing and rap music."

Importantly, young men use rap to seek social status. Often the rapper taunts his enemies, in the tradition of the griots and "the dozens," a rhymed pattern of insults long associated with the black community. The rapper intends to inspire resistance in his followers and fear in his oppressors. In a best-case scenario his boasts are sufficient to cause his enemies to withdraw in a "cost-free victory." In a worst-case scenario the words of the rapper, as of the griot, bring a people to war.

When rap first emerged from hip-hop culture and gained national attention, it often carried the sound of war and violence. Lyrics that celebrated killing cops and hating women offended critics of rap, but what critics must remember is that the violence and war did not begin with rap; instead, it began with the 17th-century slavers who disrupted the connective fabric of an ancient continent.

Black slaves brought forcibly to the New World from their native Africa were deliberately separated from their family members; children were taken from their parents, and women from their husbands. To maintain a focus on the dominance of white culture, slaves were restrained from retaining open connections with their own culture. They were allowed to congregate with other blacks from widely scattered points in Africa and the New World, rather than with their own flesh and blood. None but the most shallow of community ties were expected to develop as a result. But African Americans struggled to maintain the cultural bonds that gave them personal identity, and they adapted to the dignity-destroying chains of slavery by creating new ways to connect with others of African blood.

Religion, with its focus on the transformational power of suffering, provided a focus for African culture. Many African Americans adopted Christianity, investing in their preachers the dignity and attention previously given to the griot. To this day African-American preachers like the Reverend Jesse Jackson exhort their followers to forge a better community in America. Congregations respond to the call of their preacher—as villages once responded to the call of their storyteller—in a patterned, rhymed, rhythmic language instantly recognizable as a root of rap music. Spirituals were created, often adapting the melodic structure of European music to the rhythm of Africa. With their expressive, sorrowful melodies, yet hopeful themes, spirituals expressed the raw experience of the black slave in American history.

Still other African slaves combined Christianity with the worship of Nigerian and Yoruban gods in a fusion known simply as voodoo. Like rap, voodoo reached across the boundaries separating Africans and connected them. It created a rigid hierarchy that structured slave communities beyond and around the reaches of the European owners. A slave who was of no account to his owner during the long day of labor could be a priest at night, a leader in a like-minded community. Practitioners inspired fear in black and white communities alike, galvanizing the critics of their time to reject voodoo, much as rap would later be rejected. The messages of voodoo, like rap, were drum driven. As Gary O. Clement remarks, "The music of the drum is perpetually and unmistakably reflected in our music." The drums were a link to a lost culture and a forbidden form of communication, and the rhythm was a reminder to whites that the oppressed were still there and still resisting.

The practice of voodoo was vigorously suppressed throughout America, although it remains in a few places to this day. But the African spiritual thrived and evolved, laying the groundwork for American music of the 20th century. So did the black musical form called the blues. This musical genre developed after the Civil War, when the promises of the slavery-ending Emancipation Proclamation were rarely kept and the life of many blacks remained hard and poverty-stricken. The blues endured as the expression of the poor man's life until rap music evolved a hundred years later.

The blues clearly developed from the storytelling tradition of Africa. As Clement comments, "The music was at times rough and rude, but it could also be eloquent, poetic, and sensitive. Though it was snubbed as lowlife music, the storytelling aspect of the lyrics emphasized the facts of African-American life at that time." The blues told of "being poor and black in white America," much as rap does today.

From stomping, hand-clapping African rhythms came the upbeat music of freedom—the complex polyrhythmic, syncopated style of ragtime, popular until the 1920s. The newfound exploration of freedom also discovered a voice in jazz. Daring young people, including some whites, met to dance and celebrate the power of the beat. African Americans invested an almost religious fervor in their music, and it drew both criticism and admiration. But their music always, as now, drew attention. Like the later

R&B of the 1950s and 1960s, the music celebrated a black identity.

There was a tension between the confident self-expression achieved by urban forms of black music, such as ragtime or the funk of the 1960s and 1970s, and the pain and eloquence of the more rural blues. These conflicting types of African-American music were to be powerfully joined with the emergence of rap in the late 1970s. Teenagers of all races converged to hear the fast-moving sound, which articulated alienation from the mainstream power structure, and to form new ways to dress and act and communicate. Just as voodoo did, rap caused an alternate power structure to gain strength in African-American communities.

2

The Birth of Contemporary Rap Music

IN 1979 RAP MUSIC emerged from hip-hop culture, a renaissance of urban black creativity in the depressed Bronx district of New York City. Hip-hop was first and foremost a youth movement. Hip-hoppers embraced and demanded change; they were ready for new sounds, new dances, new clothing, new language, and an aggressive new style. The young people had non-Eurocentric views to express, and they developed their own unique mediums to do it. From those mediums—the new "turntabling," or manipulation of records, break dancing, and graffiti—rap music emerged.

Unlike many cultural phenomena, often built on financial success and educational improvements in a community, hip-hop culture developed from the voices of the city. In fact, hip-hop may have had its genesis in the destruction of a community. Many point to New York City's controversial Cross-Bronx Expressway Project, which destroyed multiethnic communities in its path, as

Children play among the ruins of Bronx homes torn down in 1977. As a result of the Cross-Bronx Expressway Project, some 170,000 people were relocated. Hip-hop culture—identified by its graffiti, break dancing, and rap music—emerged in this neighborhood during these grim years.

17

one of the most significant factors in the formation of hip-hop culture.

The Cross-Bronx Expressway Project was the brainchild of city planner Robert Moses, hired by the city of New York to oversee "urban renewal." In the neighborhood of the South Bronx his efforts at "renewal" in fact supported the interests of the city's rich, rather than those of the poor and working classes. Professor Tricia Rose says that the Cross-Bronx Expressway Project, like many of Moses's city projects, broke up black and Latino communities and left them with little leadership or resources.

Throughout the 1960s and early 1970s some 60,000 Bronx homes were torn down. By labeling these blue-collar housing units "slums," the Title I Slum Clearance Program forced the relocation of 170,000 people. These people, disproportionately nonwhite, became in effect refugees from their city planners.

In this cauldron of frustration and broken dreams, hip-hop culture was forged. To re-create a sense of community, hip-hoppers began building alternative connections. About the South Bronx, Professor Rose comments, "North American Blacks, Jamaicans, Puerto Ricans, and other Caribbean people with roots in other postcolonial contexts reshaped their cultural identities and expressions in a hostile, technologically sophisticated, multiethnic, urban terrain." They reshaped their identities into hip-hop—and from hip-hop, rap was born.

Hip-hop developed as part of an unconscious attempt to restore cross-cultural communication in a climate that marginalized the lives and opinions of young people of color. Graffiti-tagged trains became unwitting cultural ambassadors, showcasing hip-hop throughout New York City. And African-American and Latino teens from neighborhoods across the city descended on parks and clubs in the Bronx to hear rap musicians relate experiences overlooked by mainstream media and entertainment.

From the beginning there were three main elements of the hip-hop culture, which fused and refused in fantastic variety: graffiti, break dancing, and rapping. Each form of hip-hop culture expressed a personal as well as a community style. As Professor Rose notes, in the rubble of neighborhood demolition "alternative local identities were forged in fashions and language, street names, and most important, in establishing neighborhood crews or posses. . . . Identity in hip-hop is deeply rooted in the specific, the local experience, and in one's attachment to and status in a local group or alternative family."

These hip-hop crews were mistaken by the world at large for gangs. Break-dancers were often arrested when their dancing was reported as brawling. Gangs did in fact adopt the tagging style of graffiti artists to post their territory and proclaim their own answers to the process of dispossession. This fact made it difficult for hip-hop graffiti artists to achieve the legitimacy that rappers and break-dancers later achieved in American culture at large.

Young hip-hoppers increased the controversy surrounding their image. They adopted, consciously or unconsciously, a style of baggy clothing that had originated in the prison system. Men in jail were not allowed to wear belts with their pants, and consequently their pants hung down low. Hip-hoppers began wearing their pants this way, and so did break-dancers, who found the baggy pants necessary to perform their adventurous dance moves. The style was also an extension of the rebellion that hip-hop represented.

Break dancing was a dangerous style of dancing in which dancers used their entire body in complex, risky moves. Often dancers would spin on the ground on their back, shoulders, or head. Or they would even dive or fall to the ground, landing on their hands or back. Perhaps due to the risky nature of the moves and the frequent injuries that resulted from them, break dancing eventually faded from hip-hop culture.

As dancing in hip-hop culture evolved, electric-boogie moves became popular as well. This type of dancing was characterized by jerky movements as dancers twitched their muscles to the rhythm of the music. The most well known example of electric boogie is Michael Jackson's signature move, the Moonwalk. Dancers at parties all over America picked up on the electric-boogie style.

Freestyle, which emphasized improvisation, began to gain popularity by 1982. Freestyle dancers drew on, but were not limited to, the work of break-dancers and electric boogiers. All of these energetic dances required loose clothing.

But regardless of negative impressions, hip-hop was the catalyst for the re-forming of broken community connections. It underwent that process in the masterful hands of graffiti crews, break-dance crews, and the disc jockeys (DJs) who perfected the technological innovations that supported rapping.

Several DJs from the Bronx shared its major territories. Like graffiti and break-dance crews, which competed against one another for status and converts, the disc jockeys also developed their own loyal followers. The competition of hip-hop culture pushed its followers to innovate at a fantastic rate. The most successful DJs are credited with creating the staples of rap's technological base and forging its essential connections.

From its birth in the public parks of the Bronx, rap began as a way to engage party goers on the dance floor. In fact, hip-hop music as we know it began when a DJ named Kool Herc saw crowds go crazy when he played the instrumental break of a song over and over by cutting back and forth between identical copies of a record on two turnta-

This dancer gets set to perform the headspin, one of break dancing's most impressive moves. During the early '80s, break dancing caught on as rap music slowly received a more mainstream audience.

bles. This technique was called break-beat disc jockeying, and it became the core of hip-hop. By isolating and repeating the breaks of funk records, Herc created the model for modern hip-hop music. Breaks are certain nonvocal sections of funk songs, in which the exposed instrumental rhythms create exceptionally danceable segments. Though other DJs soon used and elevated the technique, Kool Herc is credited with its creation.

Kool Herc was of Afro-Caribbean heritage. He was born in Kingston, Jamaica, with the given name of Clive Campbell. He moved to the Bronx in 1969. His father played in a reggae-soul band and kept the band's sound system in Kool Herc's room. Rap music may be forever thankful for this storage solution.

Kool Herc brought the Jamaican style of disc jockeying to the Bronx. In Jamaica, DJs had started reciting improvised rhymes over records. Kool Herc did these recitations over the breaks in funk records.

Kool Herc, along with other DJ's from the Bronx, helped develop a style of disc jockeying that would become the musical foundation over which rap lyrics were laid.

Because these instrumental and percussive breaks were usually short, he used an audio mixer and two identical records to continuously replace the desired portion.

The recitations themselves were heavily influenced by the Jamaican style of "toasting," or shouting in time to the music. Rap music is the American cousin of this Jamaican party music. American rap music relied primarily on the beat of funk songs, whereas Jamaican toasting was supported by the heavy beat of Jamaican reggae. Both rappers and toasters spoke their lines in time with the music, giving their words a rhythmic quality.

Another DJ, Afrika Bambaataa, picked up on Herc's style and began rocking parties of his own. Born Kevin Donovan, Bambaataa has been called both the godfather of hip-hop and the greatest DJ on Earth. Previously a member of one of the largest gangs in the South Bronx, the Black Spades, he outgrew his gang persona and began to have a tremendous influence on rap music and hip-hop culture.

As a teen, Bambaataa saw a film called *Zulu*, which depicted the battle between British troops and the Zulu tribe in southern Africa in 1879. The name Afrika Bambaataa, meaning "affectionate leader," comes from the 19th-century Zulu leader who led his tribe to victory. Bambaataa was so moved by the film that he decided to form his own Zulu nation. He planned to try to unify young people through competition in art, dance, and music, as an alternative to gang fights on the streets. To this end, Bambaataa founded Zulu Nation in 1975. Its primary function was to replace gang fighting and drugs with rap, dance, and other forms of hip-hop style. It is ironic, then, that hip-hop has

often been mistaken for a promotion of gang violence, given Bambaataa's heroic intent.

In his role as a DJ, Bambaataa organized break-
dancing competitions and huge block parties, which
spread his message. He also began a recording career,
which in 1982 took him to the top of the charts with
his hip-hop classic "Planet Rock." Considered one of
the most influential songs of its era, "Planet Rock"
fused the popular European techno sound with the
funk and rap of Afrocentric communities. Rap
always combines its storytelling with sonic power,
and Bambaataa helped create that connection.

DJ Grandmaster Flash laid down another foundation of hip-hop tracks by taking Kool Herc's
break-beat techniques to a new level. The sounds of
hip-hop culture were influenced by Grandmaster
Flash's Afro-Caribbean heritage. He was born
Joseph Saddler in Barbados and started spinning
records as a teenager in the Bronx, performing at
local dances and block parties. By 1977 he was starting partnerships with rappers. One group—Melle
Mel (Melvin Glover), Cowboy (Keith Wiggins),
Kid Creole (Nathaniel Glover), Mr. Ness (Eddie
Morris), and Rahiem (Guy Williams)—were called
the Furious Five. The Furious Five were command-
ing rappers, most noted for their signature trading
and blending of lyrics. With Grandmaster Flash's
skill as a DJ, his crew quickly became famous
throughout New York City.

Over a period of time Grandmaster Flash developed many groundbreaking techniques. One is "cutting," or moving between tracks exactly on the beat.
He also used "backspinning," which is manually
turning records to repeat brief fragments of sound.
"Punch phasing," another technique, involves hitting a particular break on one turntable while the
record on another turntable is still playing. It is used
to accentuate the beat and rhythm for a dancing
crowd. Like many of the techniques of live rap

Afrika Bambaataa, a famous DJ and considered by many to be the godfather of hip-hop. In 1975, Bambaataa formed the Zulu Nation, a group of young people committed to rap and dance as an alternative to drugs and gang violence.

music, punch phasing is used to convey a sense of immediate energy.

Grandmaster Flash also enhanced a technique invented by an 11-year-old named Theodore: the famed "scratching" of phonograph recordings. Scratching involves spinning a record backward and forward very fast while the needle is in the groove, allowing the record to be used as a percussion instrument. Scratching demonstrates very clearly the ability of the hip-hop culture to adapt materials to new purposes.

These turntable techniques became the backbone of rap's supporting sound. During the instrumental breaks, live, spontaneous situations were created and manipulated by gifted DJs. For example, during an artificially created, extended break in a recording DJs talked to the gathered crowd, often singling out individuals by name and giving them status and inclusion. DJs used existing recordings to produce or express a new composition from the fusion of various older materials. This is how the practice of sampling evolved, in which DJs and hip-hop musicians use sections of an older recording as a foundation for a new rap. These techniques also demonstrate the philosophy of rap, which adapts earlier music to a newer, more Afrocentric expression. The techniques themselves are unique in music history.

Afrika Bambaataa, Grandmaster Flash, and Kool Herc pioneered the sounds of rap from their disc jockey positions in the South Bronx. In their hands the music merged into an expression of a local culture hungry for new connections and eager to form a unique identity. But rap music alone of the three primary elements of hip-hop culture—break dancing, grafitti, and rap—outgrew the local and burst on to the national scene, drawing in young white teenagers as well as others of the African-American diaspora. The mechanism for disseminating the message was Sugar Hill Records.

Sugar Hill was an independent record label founded in Englewood, New Jersey, by Joe and Sylvia Robinson, music business veterans. Sylvia herself was a singer, with hits such as 1957's "Love is Strange" and 1973's "Pillow Talk." In 1979 she and Joe found a new sound to promote, releasing "Rapper's Delight," the first commercially successful rap single.

The Robinsons' "discovery" of rap music is legendary. Sylvia said that she first heard the sound of rappers coming from the stereo in her son's room. She was so excited by the new, fantastic sound that she wouldn't rest until she had rearranged Sugar Hill Records to promote it and formed the band The Sugarhill Gang to record "Rapper's Delight."

Besides "Rapper's Delight," a nonsense rhyme, Sugar Hill also released the antidrug rap "White Lines." In 1982 the label released Grandmaster Flash and the Furious Five's legendary hit single "The Message." In the song Melle Mel delivers a fiery rap detailing the grim existence of life in the South Bronx ghetto. This was the first time that a prominent rap song became a vehicle for true social opinions, rather than merely bragging or boasting. The record was a major critical success, and it was a tremendous step toward highlighting rap as an important form of musical expression.

Rap's audience soon began growing. In 1982 Afrika Bambaataa and his newly formed group, the Soulsonic Force (comprised of Jazzy Jay, Mr. Biggs, Glove, and Pow Wow), released "Planet Rock." Its inventive techno sound revolutionized dance music, and its popularity sent them on a whirlwind world tour. Suddenly, hip-hop was on a global stage.

Break-dancers had already been performing overseas. Before "Planet Rock" exploded in 1983, Bambaataa, graffiti artists Dondi, Futura 2000, and Fab 5 Freddy, and the Rock Steady Crew—a break-dancing crew—all participated in the first-ever hip-hop tour, sponsored by French radio station Europe1. A Paramount Pictures executive spotted the members of the tour at a performance at the Roxy in New York and requested their participation in the film *Flashdance*. The 1983 film turned millions of kids worldwide on to break dancing and was followed the next year by a pair of movies specifically about the new urban dance genre, *Breakin'* and *Breakin' 2: Electric Boogaloo*.

The graffiti element of hip-hop culture was

An innovator on the turntables, Grandmaster Flash was one of the first DJs to form a rap group. In 1982 Grandmaster Flash and the Furious Five released "The Message," one of the first rap songs to become a major radio hit.

documented in two films of the era, Charlie Ahearn's low-budget film *Wild Style* in 1982, and Henry Chalfont and Tony Silver's 1983 documentary, *Style Wars*. *Wild Style* depicted the tradition of breaking into train yards to create graffiti art, which was considered vandalism by the rest of society. In the early 1980s graffiti moved from subway trains and inner-city walls to trendy art galleries as acceptance of hip-hop expression began to build.

With audiences exposed to hip-hop's three main elements—graffiti, break dancing, and rap music—it wasn't long before the hip-hop movement began to sweep the nation.

3

Early Promoters and Successes

Run-DMC (pictured are Joey "DJ Run" Simmons, Jason "Jam Master Jay" Mizell, and Darryl "DMC" McDaniels) was one of the most influential rap groups of the 1980s. They developed a bare-bones style of rap known as hard core, along with setting a hip-hop fashion standard with their gold chains and Adidas sneakers. Raising Hell, released in 1986, was the first rap album to go platinum.

AT THE DAWN OF the 1980s hip-hop eased into its toddler years after the success of the Sugarhill Gang's "Rapper's Delight" in 1979. A few gifted promoters guided rap through its early childhood. Two men in particular were responsible for discovering some of rap's early successes and taking them to the music marketplace: Russell Simmons and Rick Rubin. They helped explore rap's potential as they moved it from a novelty market to the mainstream.

In 1975 Russell Simmons, a native of the Hollis section of Queens, New York, graduated high school and promptly enrolled as a sociology major at the City College of New York in Harlem. He was already a music lover, never missing a chance to catch concerts by the Dramatics, Delfonics, Temptations, and other R&B bands, and soon Simmons was spending more time in Harlem's nightclubs than in classes. On a pivotal night in 1977 at the Charles Gallery, a club on 125th Street near the Apollo Theater, Simmons saw Eddie Cheeba for the first time. Cheeba, a student from Bronx Community College, grabbed the mike and unleashed a slang-filled rhyme to the beat. Simmons, along with the others in attendance, was mesmerized.

In 1984 Russell Simmons (above) founded Def Jam Records with Rick Rubin. Simmons was one of rap's original promoters; he signed such major artists as LL Cool J, Run-DMC, and Public Enemy.

Meanwhile, Cheeba's DJ, Easy Gee, was using two turntables to keep the first eight bars of "Flashlight"—a song by the funk group Parliament—going. Simmons was hooked. He took notice of the hyped crowd and started to see the moneymaking possibilities in rap music.

That fall Simmons threw his first party. Putting up $500 to rent out the Renaissance Theatre in Queens, and using $300 for promotion, he organized the bash under the name Rush. (Friends had given him this nickname for the way in which he rushed through daily routines.) From watching the crowd react to Cheeba's rhyming, Simmons knew the success of the party would depend on finding a rapper. He looked no further than one of his best friends, Kurtis Walker, a communications major at CCNY. Simmons replaced Kurtis's last name with "Blow," and the unknown Kurtis Blow rocked all 800 guests packed into the theater.

Simmons and Blow began a rapid rise in popularity, Simmons as the premier college-party thrower and Blow as an MC (short for "master of ceremonies"). Soon, Simmons had Blow sharing the stage with such popular Bronx acts as Lovebug Starski, Grandmaster Flash and the Furious Five, and Grand Wizard Theodore. When Blow needed a DJ, Simmons looked to his own home to fill the need. He chose his 13-year-old younger brother Joey, who had been honing his craft on turntables, as well as rhyming. Billed as Kurtis Blow's Disco Son DJ Run (the nickname came from the way he would "run" his mouth), Joey took advantage of his debut. He seized the microphone to rap onstage along with Blow while Grandmaster Flash manned the turntables.

Soon, throwing parties became commonplace, and Simmons looked to capitalize on the roster of rap talent he had at his fingertips. He began to manage Kurtis Blow. In 1980 Simmons tapped the writing skills of Billboard reporters Robert "Rocky" Ford and J. B. Moore to pen Blow's first single, "Christmas Rappin'." When Mercury Records came on board, history was made, as "Christmas Rappin'" became the first rap single to be distributed by a major label.

DJ Run watched Kurtis Blow follow up his debut with "The Breaks" in 1980, and he began to bug his brother to let him record a single as well. His first attempt, called "Street Kid," was a failure.

Kurtis Blow helped put hip-hop on the map with his 1980 hit single "The Breaks" and was one of the first rap artists to sign with Def Jam Records. The 1986 film Krush Groove featured a performance by Kurtis Blow, along with footage of Run-DMC and the Beastie Boys.

For his next effort Run hooked up with a neighborhood friend, Darryl McDaniels (nicknamed DMC), who also rapped. Run and Darryl asked their friend Jason Mizell (who called himself Jam Master Jay) to scratch records as their DJ. When Simmons saw his brother was serious, he decided to create a sound that would challenge the smooth, R&B-flavored bass lines suffused in the hip-hop beats from Joe and Sylvia Robinson's Sugar Hill label. Simmons wanted to begin focusing on the hard-core break-beat sounds coming from the parks. He recruited Larry Smith, the bass player on Kurtis Blow's hits, and they made a stripped-down drum track to accent Run and Darryl's rhymes. The result was the hard-hitting song "It's Like That," with "Sucker MCs" on the B side of the single. Simmons shopped the record to major labels, but no one was willing to take a chance on the new, raw sound.

Luckily, that wasn't the end of the road. Like a ray of sunshine, a small independent label, Profile Records, which had already made some money off of "Genius Rap," by Dr. Jeckyll and Mr. Hyde, agreed in 1983 to distribute the record. Suddenly the two teenagers from Hollis Queens found themselves selling 20,000 copies a week of "It's Like That" under their name, Run-DMC. The single sounded like no other rap record at the time. Run and DMC would finish each other's rhymes in an overlapping fashion. "It's Like That" became a Top 20 R&B hit, as did their follow-up single, "Hard Times," with "Jam Master Jay" on the B side. In 1984 they followed with the singles "Rock Box" and "30 Days." Finally, Run-DMC's self-titled debut LP was released later that year.

Meanwhile, in his dorm room at New York University, a 20-year-old Jewish film student from Lido Beach, Long Island, named Rick Rubin was heavily into the rap scene. Musically, Rubin craved anything alternative and progressive, from rap to the budding hard-core punk scene to James Brown and the blues.

Rubin eventually hooked up with the innovative Bronx DJ Jazzy Jay, who took him even deeper into the underground hip-hop scene in New York. Rubin yearned to make innovative rap records like the ones from his favorite group, Run-DMC. In 1984 he approached Jay with the idea of making a record and starting a label. Rubin wanted Special K of the Treacherous Three to record the rap, but K was contractually tied to Sugar Hill Records. K suggested they use his brother, T La Rock. Rubin and

Jay went to PowerPlay Studios with rapper T La Rock and recorded "It's Yours." The single was released and sold 90,000 units, making it a local hit. Even though the song was distributed by Arthur Baker's Streetwise/Partytime label, Rubin placed the name Def Jam on the single, along with the address of his dorm room. Def Jam was the name he wanted to use should he ever build a record label.

When it was time to get paid for the success of the record, Rubin was dissatisfied with the distribution of the profits. Feeling he had been cheated, Rubin pressed on with dreams of starting his own Def Jam label.

It was inevitable that Rick Rubin and Russell Simmons would eventually meet. Both were staples of the New York club scene. Already an enthusiastic fan of Run-DMC, Rubin admired the work of Russell Simmons, who by 1984 had established his own management company, Rush Management. His roster featured Run-DMC, Kurtis Blow, Whodini, Dr. Jeckyll and Mr. Hyde, Jimmy Spicer, Spyder D, Sparky D, and singer Alyson Williams.

Russell Simmons was an equally big fan of the single "It's Yours." He was initially shocked that the man behind the Def Jam imprint was white. However, the mutual fans became close friends and began to hit the club scene together.

Meanwhile, hundreds of demo tapes were pouring into Rubin's dorm room because of the address printed on the "It's Yours" single. While lounging in the room one day, he happened to hear the a cappella demo of a 15-year-old kid from St. Albans, Queens, who called himself Ladies Love Cool James. The song, aptly titled "I Need a Beat," impressed Rubin so much that he immediately brought the kid in to record the song with a beat Rubin produced himself. He played the finished product for Simmons, who thought the single was strong enough to take to Profile Records, the label that was distributing Simmons's records at the time. However, the bad experience with the Streetwise/Partytime label had left a bitter taste in Rubin's mouth. He suggested they put "I Need a Beat" out on their own. Although Simmons was reluctant at first, Rubin eventually convinced him to take a chance.

Each of them contributed $2,500 to start Def Jam Records. In November of 1984 "I Need a Beat" from Ladies Love Cool James (shortened to LL Cool J), became the first official 12-inch single released by Def Jam Records. The single eventually sold 100,000 copies, and suddenly LL Cool J was a superstar at the age of 15.

LL Cool J was not Rubin's only significant discovery. Earlier, three white teenagers in a hard-core punk band called the Beastie Boys were looking for a DJ to perform their rap-flavored single, "Cookie Puss," during live performances. Rubin agreed to the gig and simultaneously saw something in the three that might prove marketable. He took Ad Rock, Mike D, and MCA into the studio to produce three songs, "Beastie Crew," "Party's Gettin' Rough," and "Rock Hard."

Def Jam followed the success of the LL Cool J single with the release of the Beastie Boys tracks in December. Soon, Rush Management artists were climbing the charts. Whodini had the singles "Friends," "Freaks," and "Five Minutes of Funk." Kurtis Blow was continuing to churn out hit records, and Run-DMC released their first LP on Profile Records. Simmons secured a deal to supply all of the talent for Fresh Fest, the country's first major rap concert tour. Rick Rubin and Russell Simmons were well on their way to building a rap empire.

From his NYU dorm room Rubin made the records, organized the deals to press the records, designed the artwork, and worked with the distributors. Simmons's main task was to promote, promote,

promote. Often out until five in the morning, visiting up to three clubs a night, Simmons kept an ear on what records were generating the most crowd reaction, scouted out the latest musical styles, and kept abreast of the ever changing hip-hop culture from the front line. The only goal left for Def Jam was to secure a distribution deal with a major label.

Still wary of hip-hop's longevity and ability to generate profits, nearly every major label turned down Rubin and Simmons for a distribution deal. Then, in 1985, CBS Records head Al Teller approached them after realizing that seven of Def Jam's releases had sold over 250,000 units. The two signed a distribution deal with CBS that was reportedly worth more than $1 million. Under the terms, Rubin and Simmons had complete creative control. CBS's only role was pressing and distributing the records Def Jam gave them—as is. The first single released with CBS distribution was "She's on It," by the Beastie Boys, followed by LL Cool J's *Radio* album, both produced by Rubin. In 1986 Run-DMC's album *Raising Hell*, released on Profile, became the first rap album to go platinum, as well as reach number one on the R&B chart. Its success was fueled largely by its first single, a cover of Aerosmith's 1976 hit "Walk This Way."

The song almost didn't make it on the album, according to Rick Rubin. After *Raising Hell* was completed, Rubin felt there was still something missing. He thought the group should cover a song, and he promptly rifled through his extensive collection of albums to find the perfect one. When he came across Aerosmith's "Walk This Way," he realized the vocals to the 1970s rocker were already done in a rap style. Rubin felt it would shock everyone to have a hard-core rap group record a traditional rock 'n' roll song, without having to alter the song too radically. Aerosmith joined Run-DMC in the studio to rerecord the song.

The mind-blowing success of the single was a slap in the face to critics who felt that rap music was a passing fad. "Walk This Way" became hip-hop's first Top 5 pop single, and it dominated the airwaves for the entire summer of 1986. It made Run-DMC the first rap act to receive extensive airplay on MTV. Run-DMC's *Raising Hell* tour sold out arenas throughout the country. Soon to follow was the Def Jam–produced film *Krush Groove*, featuring music performances by Run-DMC, LL Cool

J, Kurtis Blow, the Beastie Boys, and other Rush Management artists.

With the signing of political rap group Public Enemy in 1987 and R&B singer Oran "Juice" Jones, Def Jam soon became responsible for approximately 70 percent of sales in Columbia's black music division. However, storm clouds began to loom overhead. The first major setback was the loss of the Beastie Boys, who left in the fall of 1987 over a dispute involving their royalty checks. After selling 4 million copies of *Licensed to Ill* and coming off a successful tour, the group expected to receive big paychecks. But according to Mike D, Simmons told the group that no money would come until another record was recorded. That prompted the Beastie Boys to leave Def Jam. They eventually signed with Capitol Records to release the critically acclaimed 1989 album *Paul's Boutique* and 1992's *Check Your Head*.

Also at this time, Rick Rubin was becoming disillusioned with the musical direction of the company and the direction of rap in general. He and Simmons were no longer seeing eye to eye. In November 1990 Rubin told *Rolling Stone*, "Musically, our tastes were different for a long time. I was responsible for LL Cool J, the Beastie Boys. At that time, Russell had brought in mostly R&B stuff, Oran 'Juice' Jones, Alyson Williams. We each ran our own team, really, but then things were starting to cross over, and when he would question what I was doing—'Why are you doing Public Enemy?'— it was becoming frustrating."

It wasn't long before Rubin and Simmons parted ways. In 1988 Rubin went out to Los Angeles to work on the soundtrack to the film *Less Than Zero* and never returned. He eventually went on to start Def American Records. Simmons renegotiated his Def Jam distribution deal. In 1990 he became an equal partner with CBS, which was now owned by Sony.

Although Simmons and Rubin eventually split, they had already put their personal stamps on the development of rap music. Together the two promoters were primarily responsible for moving rap music from the local party scene to the national arena during its first decade.

4

Rap Artists Take Center Stage

RAP MUSIC OWED a lot to promoters like Russell Simmons and Rick Rubin, but it owed even more to its artists. The wordsmiths of rap familiarized America with youthful black and urban perspectives. The names of these rap artists now read like an honor roll of music history.

By the mid-1980s, Run-DMC had taken over the rap scene with their new style of bad-boy toughness, reflected in their hits "It's Like That" and "Sucker MCs." Once the group had ushered in the new street-oriented, beats-and-rhymes style of hip-hop, the floodgates were open to rappers that would build upon the foundation laid by the Sugar Hill and Def Jam artists. They would eventually take rap into multiple directions.

During these years a host of MCs would emerge to build upon rap's early intention of rocking a crowd. Popular rappers such as Doug E. Fresh, Slick Rick, the Fat Boys, Dana Dane, Nice & Smooth, Salt-N-Pepa, MC Lyte, Heavy D, Leaders of the

KRS-One began his career as leader of the rap group Boogie Down Productions. Like Public Enemy, which arrived on the scene around the same time, KRS-One suffused his lyrics with politically conscious messages.

In 1989 Kool Moe Dee became the first rapper to perform at a Grammy Awards ceremony. In his lyrics Dee maintained a longstanding rivalry with LL Cool J that was most visible in his 1987 album How Ya Like Me Now.

New School, Big Daddy Kane, Kool Moe Dee, and LL Cool J mostly kept their rhymes centered on braggadocio and moving bodies on the dance floor.

Kool Moe Dee emerged as a solo artist with the 1986 single "Go See the Doctor." Formerly of the Treacherous Three, Kool Moe Dee later signed with Jive Records to release three successful albums: 1986's *I'm Kool Moe Dee*, 1987's *How Ya Like Me Now*, and 1989's *Knowledge Is King*. Kool Moe Dee is best known for his long-standing lyrical war with LL Cool J. Dee claims Cool J stole his rapping style. The cover of *How Ya Like Me Now* featured a red Kangol hat—the trademark of LL

Cool J—being crushed by the wheel of a Jeep. In 1989 Dee became the first rapper to perform at a Grammy Awards ceremony.

The 260-pound rapper Heavy D bounced onto the scene with lyrics about topics ranging from his weight to cultural awareness to tributes to black women. His positive image has been untainted since his 1987 debut, *Living Large*. Born Dwight Myers, Heavy was raised in the Bronx before moving with his family to Mount Vernon, New York. He began rapping at age eight, perfecting it by freestyling and writing rhymes with his high school friend Eddie F. Eventually Heavy signed with Andre Harrell's Uptown Records and released the single "Mr. Big Stuff." Two years later Heavy's second album followed, titled *Big Tyme*, with the bubbly tune "We Got Our Own Thang." *Big Tyme* eventually went platinum, but sadly, Heavy's best friend and group member Trouble T-Roy died in a freak accident while the group was on tour. Heavy dedicated his 1991 follow-up album, *Peaceful Journey*, to T-Roy's memory.

It wasn't long, however, until a new, violence-filled genre of rap hit the streets. Many rappers started focusing on the persistent gang problem still rampant in the inner cities. The rappers who filled their rhymes with tales of gang life and street hustles became known as gangsta rappers. The gangsta rappers spoke with raw voices to the young and disaffected, trailing controversy in their wake. And young Americans listened, if record sales were any guide, just as teenagers in the Bronx had responded at the beginning of hip-hop.

Schoolly D's 1985 single, "PSK What Does It Mean," is credited as the first gangsta rap record in hip-hop. The single was innovative for its echoing beat as well as its rhymes about a Philadelphia gang called the Parkside Killers. On his self-titled 1986 debut album, he was one of the first to rap about popular clothing and style. Classic singles such as "Gucci Time" and "Put Your Fila's On" reflected hip-hop's early obsession with obtaining material wealth and with the often violent quest for the money to make it happen.

The Bronx-based group Boogie Down Productions (BDP) followed suit in the gangsta rap genre with the single "9mm Goes Bang" from their 1987 debut album, *Criminal Minded*. The record was considered a hip-hop milestone for its gangsta lyrics and innovative sound. Led by KRS-One (Knowledge Reigns Supreme Over Nearly Everybody) and featuring Scott La Rock and D-Nice, the group released their follow-up, *By All Means Necessary*, in the following year. The cover depicted KRS-One peering cautiously out of a window with a shotgun in hand, re-creating a famous Malcolm X photograph.

KRS-One often says, "I am hip-hop," so that folks understand how serious he is about the art form. Born Lawrence Krisna Parker, "Kris" was raised in the Franklin Men's Shelter in the Bronx. He met his future BDP partner there—Scott La Rock, who was working as a counselor. In 1984 the two formed the group Scott La Rock and the Celebrity Three, which featured Kris, Scott Levi 167, and MC Quality. Eventually Scott and Kris would break away to form the Boogie Down Crew. In 1985 they recorded a single for Sleeping Bag Records but were cheated out of their payment for the project. This prompted the duo to rename themselves Boogie Down Productions, to emphasize the importance of being artists and producers of their own music. KRS-One's versatile rhymes quickly made him one of the most influential MCs in hip-hop. Boogie Down Productions continued even after the death of Scott La Rock, who was shot and killed in 1987 while trying to break up an argument.

Kool G. Rap, along with DJ Polo, emerged in 1989 with tales of homicide and battles against the

Mafia and the police on their debut album, *Road to the Riches*, and again in 1990 on their subsequent album, *Wanted: Dead or Alive*.

In 1987 Eric B. and Rakim debuted with the rugged album *Paid in Full*, which on the title track reflected Rakim's former life as a stickup kid. Rakim is a rapper still revered today as one of the most skillful lyricists ever to grace hip-hop. It was the complexity of his rhymes, mixed with his low, monotone delivery that set him apart from his contemporaries at the time. Along with his DJ, Eric B. (Eric Barrier), Rakim (William Griffin) wove tales of life in the streets and the quest for street hustles with inspirational words rooted in his religion of Islam. These two New York natives were the first to sample heavily from James Brown, as evidenced in their classic hits "I Ain't No Joke" and "I Know You Got Soul." The duo's first three albums went gold within their release years.

While Eric B. and Rakim were into the James Brown riffs, Long Island's Erick Sermon and Parrish Smith of EPMD (Erick and Parrish Making Dollars) were becoming known for their samples of Parliament and Roger Troutman records. EPMD had four successive gold albums. Their debut in 1988, *Strictly Business*, followed by 1989's *Unfinished Business*, was chock-full of beats accented with Parliament's "Freak of the Week" and "One Nation Under a Groove," and with Roger Troutman's "More Bounce to the Ounce." Besides the distinctive production of Erick Sermon, EPMD could instantly be singled out for their fierce, no-nonsense rhyme style and delivery.

In the South the reigning presence of the Geto Boys gave the world a tough glimpse into the harsh life of Houston's Fifth Ward. Their biggest hit, "Mind Playing Tricks on Me," depicted a fictional example of the psychological stress caused by the cutthroat, unforgiving lifestyle of Houston's ghettos.

The extremes of rap music: N.W.A. exposed hip-hop's darker side, sparking national controversy with their violent attitude expressed through "gangsta rap"; Kid 'N Play brightened hip-hop's image with their clean persona and playful antics.

On the West Coast, mainstream media were crit-
icizing rappers for glorifying the region's gang
lifestyle. As crack cocaine created war zones in
America's inner cities, Los Angeles was overrun with
the country's two most notorious gangs, the Crips
and the Bloods. Several rappers came directly from
this lifestyle, only to ignore the background in their
music. Tone-Loc, who gained fame in 1989 with the
crossover hits "Wild Thing" and "Funky Cold Med-
ina," never let on about his gang past. However,
street hustler–turned–rapper Eazy-E and his group
N.W.A. (Niggaz with Attitude) were forthcoming in
transferring their lifestyle into incendiary rhymes.
With their 1988 release of *Straight Outta Compton* on
Eazy E's own Ruthless Records, Eazy, Ice Cube, Dr.
Dre, MC Ren, and DJ Yella took hip-hop by the
throat and shook it to its core with songs like "Dope
Man" and "F— Tha Police." These songs reflected
the vernacular and profanity already present in the
inner city of Los Angeles.

N.W.A.'s popularity caused a number of gangsta
rappers to follow in their footsteps, such as Compton's Most Wanted—featuring MC Eiht—Above
the Law, and Cypress Hill, a group made up of former Latino gang members.

West Coast–based gangsta rappers like N.W.A.
often used inflammatory words to demean women.
Prostitution in the inner city bred a culture of
macho posturing where women were socially
reduced to being called sluts, reflecting a lower status than their male counterparts. Some rappers promoted a pimplike persona such as that celebrated in
films that shamelessly exploited black cultural
stereotypes, such as *Superfly* and *The Mack*. These
films are often referred to as "blaxploitation" films.

During the mid-1980s Oakland-born Too Short
started adopting the pimp lifestyle in his rhymes,
which he would record onto tapes and CDs himself
and sell out of the trunk of his car. His sexually

explicit songs generated a strong underground buzz and eventually caught the attention of Jive Records, which signed him in February of 1988. His production company, Dangerous Music, helped develop other Bay Area talent such as Ant Banks, Pooh Man, and Spice 1.

In 1988 Kid 'N Play were one of the first groups to counter rap's hard-core faction with positive, message-oriented music more palatable to radio and mass audiences. With their debut album, *2Hype*, Christopher Reid and Christopher Martin developed a party style that catapulted them into films (*House Party* I and II, *Class Act*) as well as into their own Saturday-morning cartoon, the first ever to involve a rap act.

DJ Jazzy Jeff and the Fresh Prince also became superstars as a clean-cut, enunciating antithesis to the hard-edged rap happening around them. Jeff Townes and Will Smith of Philadelphia scored a hit in 1987 with their debut single, "Girls Ain't Nothing but Trouble." After the smash follow-up "Parents Just Don't Understand," it was easy in 1990 for Will Smith to parlay his G-rated image into the NBC television series *The Fresh Prince of Bel-Air*.

Another type of rap to spring up in the late 1980s was socially conscious political rap. At the NYU dorm room that served as the Def Jam office in the mid-1980s, Rick Rubin came across the demo of a former rapper named Chucky D (Carlton Ridenour), who retired from rap after his independently released single "Lies," backed with "Check Out the Radio," fizzled in sales. The demo of "Public Enemy #1," a song by Chucky D featuring Flavor Flav, was produced by Hank and Keith Shocklee. Rubin was bowled over by the 26-year-old's flow, and he called Chucky D repeatedly for months in hopes of persuading him to come out of retirement and make a record. Employed as a messenger at the time, Chuck was reluctant to jeopardize the steady income that

was supporting his wife and child. He was unwilling to reenter the rap game unless he could add something different. Rubin wouldn't take no for an answer. He ordered his promotion man, Bill Stephany, a former rap DJ who had come to Def Jam from the alternative magazine *College Music Journal* (*CMJ*), to find a way to sign Chucky D. Rubin threatened to fire Stephany if he failed.

Stephany went to Chucky with an idea that had been brewing since his days at *CMJ*. Stephany thought it was time to mesh the hard-hitting style of Run-DMC with politics that addressed black youth. Chuck liked the idea so much that he agreed to come out of retirement. He dropped the y from his first name and signed with Def Jam.

While a graphic arts major at Adelphi Univer-

Guided by the political vision of Chuck D, Public Enemy demonstrated rap's potential for social protest. The group maintained a militaristic image, flanked by fatigue-dressed soldiers called the S1Ws that demonstrated the group's allegiance to the Black Muslims.

sity, Chuck used to make flyers for a crew of mobile DJs called Spectrum City, which included producers Hank Shocklee, his brother Keith Shocklee, and Eric "Vietnam" Sadler, known collectively as the Bomb Squad. Chuck D recruited the Bomb Squad to be his production team and added another Spectrum City partner, Professor Griff, to become the group's "Minister of Information." With the addition of Flavor Flav and another local mobile DJ named Terminator X, the group Public Enemy was born. The group released their debut album, *Yo! Bum Rush the Show*, in 1987, selling more than 150,000 units. The album also set the stage for what would be known as the most revolutionary album to hit hip-hop in the genre's history.

The 1988 release of *It Takes a Nation of Millions to Hold Us Back* would cement Public Enemy as the sole group responsible for bringing political issues into the hip-hop arena. Symbolized by their logo of a silhouetted black man placed inside a shooting target, Public Enemy and the fatigues-dressed soldiers called S1Ws (Security of the First World, commanded by Professor Griff) created an image that scared mainstream audiences. Their lyrics were laced with references to minister Louis Farrakhan and Malcolm X. Chuck's voice boomed from sound systems with a force filled with the anger and frustration of a disenfranchised black youth. It was an idea whose time had come, and millions of fans were drawn to the group's unabashed passion for black empowerment. Backed by the cacophonous beats and noises from the Bomb Squad, Public Enemy's rage against the status quo continued through 1990's *Fear of a Black Planet* album and 1991's *Apocalypse 91 . . . The Enemy Strikes Black*.

With the success of Public Enemy, hip-hop was suddenly flooded with new groups that celebrated Afrocentric themes, such as Gang Starr, which emerged in 1988 with the empowerment single

"Manifest," and X Clan with their 1990 debut, *To the East Blackwards*. Believing that Islam was the most practical religion for the black man in America, Daddy O of the group Stetsasonic often let its philosophy slip into his rhymes. As a group, Stetsasonic celebrated African culture with songs like "A.F.R.I.C.A." Another group, the Jungle Brothers, also celebrated their African roots by dressing in dashikis and beads, wearing dreadlocks, and accenting their music with African rhythms and chants.

The Jungle Brothers headed a crew of hip-hop performers known as the Native Tongues, which included De La Soul, Monie Love, Queen Latifah, and A Tribe Called Quest. The collective promoted the unification of African peoples around the world. Native Tongue's crew of rappers were hip-hop's first Afrocentric, peace-loving hippies.

Surprisingly, the politically and socially conscious rap world was joined by the formerly gangster-oriented Boogie Down Productions. After his best friend, Scott La Rock, was shot during a dispute between D-Nice and another performer, KRS-One began writing socially conscious lyrics. He started calling himself "The Teacher" and promoting self-awareness and education in his lyrics, as reflected in the songs "My Philosophy," "Black Cop," and "You Must Learn." He went solo in 1993 with the release of *Return of the Boom Bap*, which many hip-hop critics equated with the groundbreaking BDP debut *Criminal Minded*.

Hip-hop was not just for men; the ladies of hip-hop soon made their presence known. The trio Sequence is credited as the first female group to make a rap album, with their 1980 release, *The Sequence*. Discovered backstage at a Sugar Hill concert in 1979, South Carolina natives Cheryl the Pearl, Angie B., and Blondie hit it big with "Funk You Up." However, funky Four Plus One, a group formed in 1976 that featured female rapper Sha

In 1995 Salt-N-Pepa won Grammys for Best Rap Duo or Group Performance. Since the group formed in the mid-1980s—at that time they were called Super Nature—they have proven to audiences that rap is not just for the men.

Rock, predates Sequence with their 1979 single on Enjoy Records called "Rappin and Rockin the House." Sugar Hill Records signed the group in 1980, and they released the classic "That's the Joint." Sha Rock eventually hooked up with Zulu Nation members Lisa Lee and Debbie Dee to form the group Us Girls.

Super Nature hit the airwaves in 1985 with "The Showstoppa," their answer to Doug E. Fresh's hit "The Show." By 1986 Cheryl "Salt" James, Sandy "Pepa" Denton, and Latoya Hanson (later replaced by Diedre "Dee Dee" Roper) as their DJ Spinderella were renamed Salt-N-Pepa and debuted with the album *Hot Cool & Vicious*, which went platinum. Salt-N-Pepa became the first female rap act to reach platinum record sales, and in 1989 they were the first to receive a Grammy nomination.

MC Lyte (Lana Moorer) was the first female rapper to push complex lyrics through the forceful delivery employed by the male rappers of the time. Her 1988 debut, *Lyte as a Rock*, featured the hit "I Cram to Understand U," a song about a guy named Sam whom she likes but eventually leaves when she finds out he has cheated on her and is addicted to crack. The lyrical depth of the album's three other hits—"Paper Thin," "10% Dis," and the title track—proved to her male counterparts that she could deliver rhymes just as tight as any man.

In the 1980s rap music had begun the difficult task of legitimization, a process that had once transformed country music into the lyric of the working class and rock 'n' roll into the voice of the young. Soon rap, the voice of black youth, would overtake all other music categories in sales and would energize American popular music.

5

Wordsmiths of the 1990s

THE 1990s SAW a profusion of rap groups in almost every imaginable genre, and many groups that included elements of multiple genres. However, the most infamous genre, gangsta rap, seemed to dominate the charts. The group N.W.A. was responsible for launching the careers of some of gangsta rap's most well known acts. The first to leave N.W.A. over financial disputes, Ice Cube went on to launch a thriving solo career. His successful 1990 solo debut, *AmeriKKKa's Most Wanted*, was produced largely by the Bomb Squad. Shortly thereafter, Ice Cube joined the Nation of Islam. In 1991 he released the critically acclaimed album *Death Certificate*. The album featured his N.W.A.-influenced street rhymes on side A, which he labeled the Death Side; he placed rhymes influenced by his new Nation of Islam teachings on side B, entitled the Life Side.

Creative differences and financial concerns caused rapper Dr. Dre to leave N.W.A. after their 1991 album *Niggaz4life*. The following year Dre helped to establish Death Row Records, which housed Snoop Doggy Dogg, Tha Dogg Pound, Nate Dogg, the Lady of Rage, Jewell, and RBX. All of these artists appeared on Dre's solo effort, *The Chronic*, an

Famous for his laid-back delivery, Snoop Doggy Dogg's career began under the guidance of former N.W.A. member Dr. Dre. After appearing on Dre's influential album The Chronic, *Snoop emerged as a star in his own right with his 1993 solo debut,* Doggystyle, *which sold over four million copies.*

In 1996 gangsta rapper Tupac Shakur was shot and killed. For years afterward, fans would remember him for his sincere and poignant lyrics. When another famous rapper, the Notorious B.I.G., was shot and killed just six months later, many voiced their concern about gangsta rap and its potentially violent consequences.

album historic for its innovative production as well as the lyrical skills of its ace rapper, Snoop Doggy Dogg, who wrote or cowrote the majority of Dre's lyrics.

Snoop Doggy Dogg, born Calvin Broadus in Long Beach, California, began rapping in junior high school. Soon he started making tapes with his friends Warren G, who spun records and produced, and Nate Dogg, who sang in the church choir. Dr. Dre, Warren G's brother, heard a tape of Snoop and quickly signed him to his newly formed Death Row record label. His first introduction to the rap game came via a guest appearance with Dre on the title soundtrack to the movie *Deep Cover*. Mesmerizing fans with his trademark laid-back flow on *The Chronic*'s "Nuthin' but a 'G' Thang" and other singles on the multiplatinum album, Snoop went on to become one of the biggest selling and most respected rappers in the history of hip-hop. His 1993 solo debut, *Doggystyle*, went multiplatinum.

One of the most well known gangsta rappers of the 1990s, Tupac Shakur began his career as a background dancer on tour with the group Digital Underground. They allowed him to drop a verse in their single "Same Song." From there Tupac went on to launch a successful solo career in 1992 with the debut of his critically acclaimed album *2pacalypse Now*. In 1993 his stark portrayal of Bishop in the film *Juice* gained him attention as a talented actor. Soon legal troubles and run-ins with the police would dominate the news. But Tupac persevered and continued to write some of the most profound words in hip-hop. Struggles with the police and several prison stints increased his gangsta persona, which by 1995 he would proudly proclaim via a tattoo on his chest that read "Thug Life." However, Tupac's lyrical depth allowed him to continue writing tender, poignant songs such as "Dear Mama" and "Keep Ya Head Up." After signing with Death Row in 1995, Tupac began a public feud with his former friend, the Notorious B.I.G., a Brooklyn rapper who was signed to Sean "Puffy" Combs's new Bad Boy label.

Notorious B.I.G., or Biggie Smalls, was following in the original gangster–Schoolly D tradition; he was known for hard-core lyrics about street life and the pursuit of material wealth. He had quite a bit of company. Songs such as "Jeeps, Lex Coups, Bimas & Benz" from Lost Boyz; "Money Ain't a Thang" from Jermaine Dupri and Jay-Z; "Touch Me, Tease Me" from Case and Foxy Brown; and "Crush on You" from Lil' Kim were filled to the brim with lyrics about acquiring $100,000 cars, expensive designer clothing and jewelry, and living in mansions. Although hip-hop has always had MCs who incorporated champagne wishes and caviar dreams into their lyrics, never before had it been so visibly a reflection of the desires of black youth.

Notorious B.I.G. displayed a lyrical depth on his

Vanilla Ice poses with his two American Music Awards in 1991. Rappers like Vanilla Ice and MC Hammer gained mainstream appeal through their fusion of rap with dance and pop music, although they were criticized by other rappers for being all style and no substance.

debut, *Ready to Die*, that was unrivaled at the time of its 1994 release. The album also contained bold tales of stickups in the song "Gimme the Loot," and innocent dreams of stardom in the album's first single, "Juicy." While Biggie was recording his second album, Tupac was shot and killed in Las Vegas, spurring rumors that the feud with Biggie somehow made him responsible. Six months later the Notorious B.I.G. was shot and killed in Los Angeles. No suspect has been arrested in either of the murders.

The dominance of gangsta rap was challenged in the 1990s by rappers targeting the dance audience. Going head-to-head with gangsta rap in the early '90s was MC Hammer, a former Oakland Athletics batboy who went on to dominate the charts with his second album, *Please Hammer, Don't Hurt 'Em,* which featured the crossover smash "U Can't Touch This." Known more for his dazzling live shows and dance numbers than for his lyrical skills, MC Hammer reaped millions with what critics and rap aficionados wrote off as all sparkle and no substance.

In a similar vein, white rapper Vanilla Ice emerged in 1991 to become the most successful entertainer since Michael Jackson. His blazing first single, "Ice Ice Baby," became the first rap single to reach number one on the pop charts, where it spent 16 weeks. Vanilla Ice, born Robert van Winkle in Miami, first hit the scene at age 22, and his debut album, *To the Extreme,* sold 7 million copies in the United States. But as quickly as his star rose, it plummeted hard once he began to alienate rap fans with his clownish outfits, his cameo role in the second *Teenage Mutant Ninja Turtles* movie, and an obviously false attempt to claim a ghetto background.

Not all the groups rivaling gangsta rap were lacking lyrical and philosophical depth. Arrested Development's 1992 debut, *Three Years, Five Months and Two Days in the Life of . . .,* which took its title from the amount of time it took the group to get a record deal, fused down-home soul and blues with hip-hop to create a progressive sound. The album garnered rave reviews, sold more than 4 million copies, and won a Grammy for Best Rap Album by a Duo or Group. Arrested Development also won a Grammy for Best New Group, becoming the first rap act to do so. Group members Speech (Todd Thomas) and Headliner (Timothy Barnwell) had met in the late 1980s while attending the Art Institute in Atlanta. They first formed a gangsta group called Disciples of Lyrical Rebellion but decided to adopt a more positive rhyme style after hearing Public Enemy. "Tennessee," the first single from their debut album, was a spiritual track inspired by the death of Speech's brother and grandmother. "Tennessee," along with its two follow-ups, "People

launching a string of gold and platinum solo spin-offs. Along with rugged lyricists like Nas, Redman, and Jeru the Damaja, the members of the Wu-Tang favored hard-core, gritty tales of street life backed with stripped-down beats created by member the RZA. Clan members Method Man, Ol' Dirty Bastard, Genius, Raekwon, Ghostface Killa, Rebel INS, Ugod, Inspektah Deck, and Masta Killa adopted the personae of the Shaolin warriors depicted in Chinese martial-arts films. Each MC had a distinctive flavor that proved successful on subsequent solo ventures. Together, their debut created a force that dented the popularity of the dominant Death Row sound of 1993.

The 1990s also featured several successful female rappers. New Jersey rapper Queen Latifah debuted in 1989, the first MC to combine three careers as a rapper, actress, and businesswoman. Her

Queen Latifah poses next to a poster of herself in a promotion for her album, Order in the Court. *An actress as well as a rapper, her credits include roles in Spike Lee's film* Jungle Fever *and the Fox sitcom* Living Single.

socially conscious debut album, *All Hail the Queen*, successfully fused rap, R&B, reggae, and house music. The album went platinum, reached number six on Billboard's R&B chart, and received a Grammy nomination.

Queen Latifah's regal persona and critical acclaim gave her the tools she needed to flex her entrepreneurial muscles. Born Dana Owens in East Orange, New Jersey, Latifah began her career when she met DJ Mark the 45 King and other members of what would become the Flavor Unit, the crew of people who recorded demos with Mark. Mark played Latifah's demo tape to an executive from Tommy Boy Records, and she was signed to the label in 1988. Her first album, 1989's *All Hail the Queen*, featured the reggae-influenced singles "Wrath of My Madness" and "Princess of the Posse," the dance beat of "Come into My House," and the feminist classic "Ladies First," a duet with Monie Love. In 1990 *Rolling Stone* readers voted her Best Female Rapper.

Shortly after the release of her second album, 1991's *Nature of a Sista'*, Latifah began to receive acting roles in films such as Spike Lee's *Jungle Fever*, Ernest Dickerson's *Juice*, and George Jackson and Doug McItenry's *House Party 2*; she also made an appearance on the television show *The Fresh Prince of Bel-Air*. In 1993 Queen Latifah's third album, *Black Reign*, was released by Motown, and Latifah and her manager, Shakim Compere, founded Flavor Unit Records. That same year, she won the role of Kaddijah on the Fox sitcom *Living Single*. Eventually, Flavor Unit would grow to become Flavor Unit Entertainment, which holds Flavor Unit Records, Flavor Unit Real Estate, and Flavor Unit Films. Latifah's latest venture is her hour-long talk show, *Latifah*, which made its debut in September of 1999.

Another example of a rapper taking advantage of her initial success is Sister Souljah's second career as a public speaker. The self-proclaimed "raptivist" spends her time lecturing young African-American women on black female empowerment.

Born Lisa Williamson in Brooklyn, New York, Souljah attended Rutgers University and became involved with the Free South Africa movement toward the end of her sophomore year. She became a regular on the college lecture circuit, traveling to more than 40 universities a year, including Harvard and Yale.

Souljah became known for her incendiary cameos in Public Enemy videos. She spent a brief time as MC Lyte's manager before joining Public Enemy full-time in 1991. She soon released the solo single "The Final Solution: Slavery's Back in Effect," followed by her 1992 album, *360 Degrees of Power*.

The album's sociopolitical views on race relations caught the ear of President Clinton. Hearing of an interview where Souljah called for African Americans to stop destroying their own property and turn their aggression on the white power structure, the president interpreted the comment as an urging of blacks to randomly target and kill whites. The controversy led Souljah to appear on numerous talk shows. Her album, however, failed to generate enough sales. Her label, Epic Records, released her from her contract, and she returned to the lecture circuit full-time. In 1995 she wrote her autobiography, *No Disrespect*. Her second book, a work of fiction entitled *The Coldest Winter Ever*, was released in March of 1999. Souljah is presently the executive director of Daddy's House Social Programs, a privately funded charity founded by rap mogul Sean "Puffy" Combs to promote educational, cultural, and recreational services to young people in New York.

Although the ladies of hip-hop started off trying to compete with the hard-core personae of the men, soon a new crop of MCs emerged that would turn female rap in a new direction. Lil' Kim and Foxy

Brown hit the scene during hip-hop's materialistic phase of the mid to late 1990s with lyrics that boasted of raw, explicit sexuality and the acquisition of all the trappings of wealth. These topics spurred controversy among critics, who felt their explicit lyrics translated into an irresponsible image detrimental to young girls. Despite the criticism, Foxy Brown and Lil' Kim expanded the tight parameters of the female's role in hip-hop.

Lauryn Hill, however, tore down the parameters altogether with her record-breaking solo debut, *The Miseducation of Lauryn Hill*, which garnered an unprecedented five Grammys for a female rap artist.

Along with the evolution of these hip-hop styles and agendas came a steady increase in the amount of money hip-hop generated per year, perhaps the best proof that black youth culture had successfully been expressed to a mainstream audience. In the late 1990s, albums by the Notorious B.I.G., the Wu-Tang Clan, Scarface, Tupac Shakur, and Wyclef Jean of the Fugees dominated the pop charts. Elektra Entertainment chairwoman Sylvia Rhone, who signed rapper-producer Missy "Misdemeanor" Elliott to the label, told the *Los Angeles Times*, "The fact is that hip-hop music is really driving the economy of the record business these days. It's the force drawing consumers into record stores." Missy Elliott's debut CD, *Supa Dupa Fly*, entered the Billboard pop chart at number three, selling 130,000 units during its first week in stores. Her album sold more during that week in 1997 than the albums of rock legends U2, Paul McCartney, Aerosmith, and Jon Bon Jovi combined in that span—all of which were released that same week. Her feat was a testament to the power and influence of hip-hop as a lucrative force in the mainstream market.

But even though 20 years of rap music have produced such a fantastic array of artists and amazing financial success, rap still continues to receive steady fire from the media for the content of its lyrics. It seems as though all rappers "[look] the same" to conservative American society, which is often unable to see that only a few rappers perpetuate a violent image.

6

Politics of an Art Form

POPULAR MUSIC HAS always flirted with threats of censorship from the U.S. government. Various artistic expressions, from paintings to literature, have been shut off from the public by a few in the federal government who find them offensive. Hip-hop music has suffered through more than its fair share of attempts to silence the voice of the artist.

The First Amendment of the U.S. Constitution gives every American the right to free speech. Specifically, it states, "Congress shall make no law respecting an establishment of religion, or prohibiting the free exercise thereof; or abridging the freedom of speech, or of the press; or the right of the people peaceably to assemble, and to petition the Government for a redress of grievances." However, the government and its moral police have had a history of challenging hip-hop artists' right to the freedom to record the lyrics of their choice, no matter how profane, violent, or sexually explicit.

In the 1980s mainstream eyes were on the growing popularity of hip-hop. Once the music began to seep into the homes of suburban white kids, many parents got wind of the bluntness with which rappers spoke of their street-hustling lifestyle

In the late 1980s and early 1990s, the rap world had numerous battles with censors. Some protested the profanity of many of the lyrics, while others felt that some songs urged its listeners toward violence, such as the 1992 single "Cop Killer" by Ice-T.

In 1985 Tipper Gore (wife of then-Senator Al Gore) led a campaign against the explicit lyrics of rap and other forms of popular music. She helped form the Parents' Music Resource Center (PMRC), which demanded that record companies provide a warning sticker with any albums containing explicit lyrics. Her opponents felt the crusade threatened the First Amendment's free speech clause.

and hate for the police.

Out of this growing concern about rap's influence on its young fans, Tipper Gore (wife of then-Senator Al Gore) helped to form the Parents' Music Resource Center (PMRC) in 1985, which lobbied record companies to rate artists' releases with a system similar to film ratings. A law was soon passed enacting this proposed system, making the "Parental Advisory, Explicit Lyrics" sticker almost synonymous with hip-hop.

In 1989 two controversial incidents in hip-hop, one in California and one in Florida, would challenge the government's strict stand on profanity, sexually explicit lyrics, and the promotion of violence in hip-hop.

The first, one of the most overt cases ever of governmental intrusion into free speech, occurred in Dade County, Florida. Police there set up a sting to arrest three retailers who were selling copies of a record by the 2 Live Crew to children under the age of 18. One of the suspects, E-C Records store owner Charles Freeman, was eventually convicted in October of 1990 on misdemeanor charges of selling the album. He was sentenced to probation and fined $1,000.

That sting was merely the tip of the iceberg. Broward County sheriff Nick Navarro led a campaign to ban the album in Fort Lauderdale and succeeded in obtaining a ruling from U.S. district judge Jose Gonzalez that the lyrics were obscene for their numerous sexual references. In his ruling Judge Gonzalez even went so far as to call the album "an appeal to dirty thoughts and the loins." However, this ruling was eventually overturned by the 11th U.S. Circuit Court of Appeals in Atlanta, which ruled that Judge Gonzalez had ignored testimony by music critics and others as to the album's artistic merit. The law's definition of *obscene* says it must seem prurient—or unwholesome—to the average person, describe sexual conduct in a patently offensive way, and lack serious artistic value. Apparently, the 2 Live Crew's music rests somewhere beyond the boundaries of the definition. Under obscenity laws, Navarro's deputies twice arrested the 2 Live Crew members during live performances, yet both times they were acquitted.

Meanwhile, 3,000 miles to the west, in Los Angeles, the other big clash between hip-hop and the government was taking place. The controversy erupted once N.W.A.'s album *Straight Outta Compton* hit the streets in 1988. The album went platinum with minimal radio play, yet it gained nationwide attention when the track "F—— Tha Police" was condemned by the 200,000-member Fraternal Order of Police and the Federal Bureau of Investigation. They felt that "F—— Tha Police" was a direct threat to their organizations as well as to law enforcement groups across the country. Priority Records, which distributed records for the label that released *Straight Outta Compton*—Eazy-E's Ruthless Records—received a letter from the FBI. The letter outlined the FBI's concerns about the lyrics that called for violence against the police. Yet hip-hop critics lauded the single for its honest expression of anger at the rampant mistreatment of young black males by police in Los Angeles. The first verse of the song underscores a pervasive feeling among African Americans about racial discrimination by the police:

> F—— tha police
> Comin' straight from the underground.
> Young niggas got it bad cuz I'm brown
> And not the other color so police think
> They have the authority to kill a minority.

Once the FBI's infamous letter to Priority Records was publicized, a massive press corps followed N.W.A. during their 50-city tour. However, the media was disappointed, as no violent incidents occurred.

This wouldn't be the last time the police protested a rap song. In 1992 Ice-T, the first West Coast artist to rap about the gangsta lifestyle, found himself the target of a censorship battle with Time Warner, the parent company of the Warner Brothers record label which distributed his albums. A song entitled "Cop Killer" was to be featured on the album by Ice-T's group, Body Count. However, the Texas Fraternal Order of Police threatened a boycott of Time Warner unless they took the song off of the album. Time Warner at first stood behind

Ice-T in defense of his First Amendment right to free speech, but the company eventually gave in, unwilling to risk the loss of hundreds of millions of dollars in the planned mass boycott. On July 28, 1992, Ice-T pulled the song from the album, which was called *Body Count*. The rapper praised Time Warner for their early support; however, the company dropped Ice-T from the label when his next album, 1993's *Home Invasion*, featured cover art they deemed too offensive.

The "Cop Killer" controversy reverberated throughout the industry, as labels bent over backward to avoid potential controversies of their own. A&M artist Tragedy had to remove the song "Bullet" from his album because it sounded too much like "Cop Killer." The Boo-Yah Tribe had to drop the song "Shoot 'Em Down" from their album for the Hollywood Basic label. Juvenile Committee had to let go of the song "Justice for the Hood," and the Almighty RSO was dropped altogether from the Tommy Boy label after their first single, "One in the Chamba," was interpreted to condone the shooting of police.

Warner Brothers artist Kool G. Rap, who had gotten away with dramatic and detailed stories of police killings and street life, suddenly had to remove every reference to violence against the police on his album *Live and Let Die—The Movie*. The reediting of the album not only compromised the release date, but it affected the album's creative vision as well. The original version played like a movie, complete with tales of G. Rap's childhood and his slip into the gang life. The album had inserts of movie reviews and voices tying the song together, which had to be cut under Time Warner's strict new guidelines.

Time Warner artist Paris, the politically conscious Oakland rapper whose album *Sleeping with the Enemy* came under fire for the songs "Bush Killa" and "Coffee, Donuts & Death," spoke out about the double standard regarding censorship. "I might not mind all this censorship so much if it didn't seem that rappers were the targets of it to a much greater extent than any other type of recording artist," Paris said at a press conference in November of 1992. "It's infuriating that Warner Music goes after me, but gives the green light and everything short of a big parade down Broadway to [Warner artist] Madonna, whose work is surely as offensive to as many people as mine is."

As Paris attempted to release his *Sleeping with the Enemy* album elsewhere, the American Civil Liberties Union's Arts Censorship Project rallied in support of "Bush Killa," a first-person fantasy narrative about a man plotting to kill the president. The group's director, Marjorie Heins, thought the song dealt primarily with political issues such as racism, police violence, and the Gulf War, and therefore could not be considered a true threat against the president.

Threats of boycotts also forced Time Warner to sever ties with the label Interscope Records, home to Death Row Records. Founders Jimmy Iovine and Ted Fields had launched Interscope in January of 1991 as a $20 million joint venture with Warner Music's Atlantic Group. Within two years the label reached domestic sales of more than $70 million with such artists as Nine Inch Nails, Primus, and 4 Non Blondes and the megasuccess of Death Row artists Dr. Dre, Snoop Doggy Dogg, and Tupac Shakur.

Chief among Time Warner's critics were C. Delores Tucker, chairperson of the National Political Congress of Black Women, and former drug czar William Bennett. They were joined by Senator Bob Dole, who also voiced his contempt for Time Warner.

In 1995 Tucker launched a full-out assault on Time Warner for distributing lyrics she felt were pornographic and detrimental to black youth. In her view gangsta rap "celebrates the rape, torture and murder of women." Tucker often quoted the violent rhymes of Tupac Shakur in her attempt to push her anti–gangsta rap agenda. Tucker's ire was directed at the "white executives" who she felt were forcing black rappers to use profanity and sexually explicit lyrics as a condition of being signed.

In direct response to Tucker's drive to boycott Time Warner until they got rid of gangsta rap, a collective of black leaders met with Time Warner executives in New York to warn of ensuing African-American protests should the company bow to conservative pressure. Among those in attendance at this historic meeting were Rev. Al Sharpton and Rev. Jesse Jackson. Both rose up in ardent support of hip-hop's creative expression. They wrote off Tucker's campaign as an example of her manipulation by the right wing. In a column for *Vibe* magazine Jesse Jackson denounced Senator Dole's support of the antirap campaign. Jackson wrote, "In railing against the lyrics of gangsta rap, Dole denounces the messengers, and slights the message. There is no excuse for some of these lyrics. But there is also no excuse for our ghettos—where young men can't find jobs [nor] support families, where hope has gone and drugs and guns become a way out."

Dole and Tucker were not the only politicians taking a long look at rap music. In 1994 the Senate had held hearings over the social impact of gangsta rap. Congresswoman Maxine Waters, a Democrat from Los Angeles who supports rap music, followed a House of Representatives subcommittee hearing on the issue by saying, "It would be a foolhardy mistake to single out poets as the cause of America's problems." Later that month Senator Carol Moseley-Braun, a Democrat from Illinois, chaired a Senate subcommittee hearing on explicit lyrics. Senator Moseley-Braun felt that record companies should

In the late 1980s hip-hop artists like the Beastie Boys were faced with copyright infringement lawsuits. Many people in the music industry questioned the legality of "sampling," when rappers insert a piece of a song into the background of their own tracks.

bear more of the blame for controversial lyrics slipping through the cracks. She said, "Those in the industry cannot dodge their responsibilities to society by hiding behind the First Amendment."

Despite the efforts of Sharpton and Jackson, Time Warner eventually buckled under the pressure and dropped Interscope Records from their label. Iovine and Fields took their label to MCA, which signed Interscope in a $200 million deal. Now Death Row would have to answer ultimately to MCA. Under this new arrangement Tupac's two-CD collection, *All Eyez on Me*, was released, with lyrics that mention a strong dislike of Tucker. However, Time Warner's noninvolvement with Interscope Records was in name only. The company secretly profited from *All Eyez on Me* after quietly securing a deal to manufacture the record, collecting $5 million in production fees from Interscope. Also, Time Warner earned hundreds of thousands of dollars in publishing fees from Death Row's new Tha Dogg Pound album, *Dogg Food,* an album the company refused to manufacture or distribute after rap critics attacked it.

Another voice joining the growing antirap sentiment was Rev. Calvin Butts, pastor of the Abyssinian Baptist Church in Harlem. Butts is best known for his public display of crushing rap tapes deemed offensive underneath a massive steamroller. Like Tucker, Butts felt that many of the gangsta rappers were being exploited by big business. During this time Butts said the following in *Black Elegance* magazine:

> Gangsta rappers, record companies and record stores should see me as the big bad parent, because I am speaking out against the violence and sexual exploitation being encouraged through the genre of pornographic music. We want to protect our children from this garbage, and I am encouraging others to get on board to stop it. If they think parents ought to become more responsible concerning what their children listen to, then my response is that I am the big parent, and all children are my children. Many people have only been talking about the exploitation in gangsta rap music, but we want to put the message out there in a very radical and militant manner.

First Amendment issues were not hip-hop's only problem with the law. Rap soon found itself inundated with lawsuits confronting its inherent phenomenon of sampling. Sampling is the electronic copying of snippets from another artist's recordings. The device has been a vital part of hip-hop since its birth in the Bronx parks. During rap's early days, when the art form was still considered to be underground, no thought was given to the legality of using break beats from other artists. Yet as rap evolved and became more visible to the mainstream, so did its blatant use of other recordings. With the increasing revenues generated by rap came

Biz Markie is known as much for his legal problems as for his achievements as a rapper. In 1991 he was the first rapper to lose a copyright infringement case concerning a sample in his song "Alone Again (Naturally)." The ruling ordered that all copies of his album I Need a Haircut, which contained the song, be removed from store shelves.

more and more frustration from artists who suddenly saw other people profiting from the use of their voices or music without permission.

Most rap lawsuits are rooted in copyright infringement, in which the original owner of a work that was sampled has been denied credit or compensation for the use of his or her piece. Under the Copyright Act of 1976 a musical recording embodies the written composition as well as the sound recording itself. Therefore, permission must be obtained from the copyright owners before a work may be reproduced.

One of the first sampling lawsuits was *Castor vs. Def Jam Records*, filed on August 25, 1987. Jimmy Castor sued the Beastie Boys' label over a drum sample and the phrase "Yo, Leroy" from his 1977 hit "The Return of Leroy (Part 1)." In 1989 De La Soul was sued for their sample of the Turtles' 1969 hit "You Showed Me" in the De La Soul song "Transmitting Live from Mars." Vanilla Ice was sued for using an unauthorized sample of Queen and David Bowie's "Under Pressure" in his hit "Ice Ice Baby." MC Hammer's "U Can't Touch This" was also targeted in court for its illegal Rick James "Superfreak" sample. All of these lawsuits were settled out of court. However, a landmark lawsuit against Biz Markie in 1991 became the first case to receive a judge's ruling.

In *Grand Upright Music Ltd. vs. Warner Brothers Records*, British pop star Gilbert O'Sullivan sued Biz's label over illegal use of his 1972 hit "Alone Again (Naturally)." Biz used the same title for his single and sampled the first eight bars, including the refrain, "Alone again, naturally." On December 16, Judge Kevin Thomas Duffy ruled in favor of

O'Sullivan. He ordered all copies of Biz's 1988 album, *I Need a Haircut,* containing the offending song, off the shelves.

By the time Biz released his next album, *All Samples Cleared,* the industry was awash with sample clearinghouses that focused all of their efforts in acquiring rights and negotiating fees. For each sample to be cleared, a publishing fee must be negotiated, as well as a fee for use of the master. Fees are determined on the basis of a statutory royalty rate set by Congress. Master use is determined more by a nominal fee.

Citing the length of time it takes to clear a sample, many producers began to bring in live musicians to re-create the sample; however, a fee for the publishing rights to the sample must still be paid. Frequently used break beats, such as those found on the Ultimate Breaks and Beats series of records, must also be cleared, yet often were not.

Some producers tried to get away with uncleared samples by burying them in layers upon layers of sounds and scratches. Producers began using more-obscure sounds in their work as a direct challenge to the sample clearance routine.

Arista Records thought they could get away with sampling Chuck D's voice in the Notorious B.I.G. song "Ten Crack Commandments," produced by DJ Premiere. Chuck filed a lawsuit against the label. He also filed a lawsuit against St. Ides malt liquor after one of their radio ads featured a sample of Chuck saying, "Incredible! Number one!"

Since the Biz Markie ruling rap producers can no longer sample with reckless abandon. Clearance fees have to be considered. Although this may hinder the creativity of the rap artist, it ensures that the original artists being sampled get their fair share of the pie.

7

Hip-Hop and the Media

CHUCK D HAS PROCLAIMED that rap is the black CNN. From its inception in public parks in the Bronx, hip-hop has been the vehicle through which the issues and interests of urban youth— including religion, street life, African culture, gangs, cars, jewelry, politics, drugs, and sex—have been explored. In an interview with *Rolling Stone*, former Def Jam head Rick Rubin summed up the notion of hip-hop as an expression of youth culture: "The reason these groups have gotten to where they are is because they weren't telling people something that didn't already exist. All they do is talk about things that are going on. They may not be pleasant, but they're real. You can't paint a pretty picture—all you can do is hold up a mirror."

Rarely has a medium been so powerful in expressing the issues relevant to the lifestyle of inner-city kids. Despite the medium's power, however, it took years before the mainstream media would acknowledge rap's popularity or validity.

Radio stations slowly warmed to rap, going from providing virtually no airplay to incorporating specialized hip-hop hours via after-dark mix shows. *The Wake Up Show*, hosted by former rappers Sway and King Tech, has been the most successful mix show

Some members of the rap community still have had violent altercations since the death of Tupac Shakur and the Notorious B.I.G. In 1998 Deric "D-Dot" Angeletti, a record producer who has worked with Puffy Combs, was arrested for attacking Jesse Washington, editor-in-chief of the hip-hop magazine Blaze.

to come along owing to its nationwide acceptance by hard-core fans. Created in 1990, *The Wake Up Show* ushered in a new era in hip-hop radio, as Sway and Tech played only underground rap records in lieu of the fare currently in heavy radio rotation.

The Wake Up Show began when King Tech's victory in a San Francisco disc jockeying competition landed him a 15-minute DJing spot on the Bay Area's KMEL radio station. The executives liked what they heard and invited him back repeatedly, until he was offered a regular slot. Tech brought in his partner, Sway, and the rest is history. *The Wake Up Show* is currently syndicated in major markets across the country. Sway and Tech continue to play unreleased tracks, stage freestyle battles, and invite underground rappers to the studio for one-on-one interviews.

It was much more difficult to get underground rap any television airtime. By 1989 MTV had just begun playing rap music in regular rotation, which greatly increased the popularity and crossover appeal of acts like Tone-Loc, MC Hammer, Young MC, and Vanilla Ice. MTV introduced *Yo! MTV Raps* in 1989, hosted by Brooklyn hip-hop connoisseur Fab 5 Freddy. The half-hour format called only for Freddy to introduce the videos, with the occasional interview of a studio guest. The show was cheap to produce and exposed more of hip-hop's underground artists to mainstream America.

Before 1984 MTV was reluctant to air music by rap artists, but public pressure had forced them to air videos from black megastars Michael Jackson and Prince. The successes of these artists would eventually open the door for the creation of *Yo! MTV Raps*. However, the early exclusion of black videos on MTV led to the emergence of other outlets that programmed hip-hop, such as the New York–based Video Music Box channel and the Los Angeles–based *Pump It Up* rap video show hosted

Many businessmen have built their enterprises on the appeal of hip-hop culture. In 1979 Robert L. Johnson founded the cable network Black Entertainment Television (BET), which for twenty years since then has showcased rap music videos as part of its programming.

by rapper Dee Barnes in 1990.

Another opportunity for audience exposure was the cable network Black Entertainment Television, founded by Robert L. Johnson in 1979. BET went on the air in January of 1980 as an advertiser-supported basic cable programming service, airing two hours a week every Friday night. It has since grown into a 24-hour showcase of black music videos, live performances, classic sitcoms, comedies, news, and public affairs. By 1998 the network was beaming into 55.5 million cable households and more than 90 percent of black cable households, according to Nielsen Media Research.

Rap City was BET's video program dedicated to hip-hop, often playing the less popular rap videos that were ignored by *Yo! MTV Raps*. However, the success and visibility of both MTV and BET made the video an integral marketing tool, along with street promotions and radio airplay. The rap music video in particular helped viewers visualize the graffiti, break dancing, and urban neighborhoods that were rapped about in hip-hop songs.

In addition to MTV and BET, the Box Music Network emerged during the '80s, offering the world's only interactive, all-music basic cable channel that catered to the musical tastes of audiences according to market. The interactive nature of the Box Music Network would serve as a precursor to the explosion of interactive websites that allow browsers to listen to live hip-hop mix shows from anywhere in the world, download the latest rap records, or purchase the latest rap albums online, directly from the artist.

Hundreds of thousands of hip-hop-oriented websites have flooded the Internet, such as the Pipeline Network, which offers live shows and album reviews. Rapweek presents weekly broadcasts of new releases and interviews. Hip-hop's Vinyl Heaven features a list of artists on CDs and vinyl for trade, as well as its own Internet radio broadcast. Chuck D and Wildman Steve host the Internet music station Bring the Noise, which features live feeds, artist interviews, and hip-hop news.

In fact, Chuck D has been an outspoken advocate of the Internet and its power to bypass traditional industry red tape. The Public Enemy front man has taken full advantage of the Internet's ability to eradicate the need to deal with record labels by choosing to sell all of his future endeavors online.

In April of 1999 Chuck signed with Atomic Pop, the Web's first full-service music company. The company boasts that their label puts artists back in control of their own music and closer to their audience. Founded by former CBS Records president Al

Teller, the Santa Monica, California–based company aims to revolutionize the way music is acquired, marketed, promoted, sold, and distributed.

In the summer of 1999 Public Enemy released their album *There's a Poison Goin' On* through Atomic Pop. It was their first studio album since 1994's *Muse Sick-N-Hour Mess Age*. The website offered three groundbreaking ways that fans could purchase the album. The first method was to buy it directly off of the website for $10 and have it shipped via mail to the buyer's home. The second method was to download the album for $8 using the a2b music player or RealNetworks' Real Jukebox. This method made Public Enemy the first multiplatinum artist to offer a full album for digital download. The third method was to buy the album on an Iomega Zip disk, a rewriteable disk that can hold nearly 100 times as much information as the traditional 3.5-inch floppy disk. Public Enemy became the first group to offer an album of any kind in Zip-disk format, which retailed at $16.98.

Ice-T signed a record deal with Atomic Pop in July of 1999. The website promoted his seventh album, *7th Deadly Sin*, in much the same manner as Public Enemy's *There's a Poison Goin' On*. Chuck D says that Atomic Pop's blend of the record game and the tech game makes it a launching pad for the new, powerful ideas that Public Enemy has in store for the 21st century.

As hip-hop fans were being introduced to this powerful new medium, the traditional media outlets were trying to counter their long history of limiting their rap music coverage by instead highlighting the violence occasionally associated with rap. Even before hip-hop was created, popular media would often portray black youth as a threat to the safety of mainstream America. Because rap music became the dominant voice of urban youth, it became a genre to fear. This pervasive wariness of hip-hop was fueled by several major violent incidents at rap concerts.

On September 10, 1988, a fight broke out at a rap show held at the Nassau Coliseum, resulting in the stabbing death of 19-year-old Julio Fuentes. The incident garnered national attention and had major ramifications on the willingness of major venues to book rap artists. The *New York Post* covered the incident with the headline "Rampaging Teen Gang Slays 'Rap' Fan." This insinuated that in some way rap was a contributing factor in the gang's motivation. The more accurate *New York Times* account described the stabbing as the result of a "robbery spree" conducted by approximately a dozen men.

The first mainstream articles on rap often focused solely on negative incidents. Reviews on the validity of the art form were mostly negative as well. *Newsweek*'s Jerry Adler criticized "the thumping, clattering, scratching assault of rap—pieced together out of pre-recorded sound bites." *Time* magazine's Janice Simpson wrote, "The lyrics, a raucous stew of street corner bravado and racial boasterism, are often salted with profanity and sometimes with demeaning remarks about whites, women and gays. The fact that they are delivered by young, self-consciously arrogant black men in a society where black youths make many whites uneasy doesn't help either."

Both of these reviews wrote off rap, calling it an invalid art form and playing in to the fear of rap and urban youth already implanted by the media in mainstream society. In her book *Black Noise*, Tricia Rose writes, "The presence of a predominantly black audience in a 15,000-capacity arena communicating with major black cultural icons whose music lyrics and attitude illuminate and affirm black fears and grievances, provokes a fear of the consolidation of black rage." Objective media reporting that respected the culture and contributions of hip-hop was greatly needed. Luckily, several

Quincy Jones, here receiving an award as Entertainer of the Year at the NAACP's 27th Image Awards in 1996, has helped expand the black entertainment world over the years. In 1993 he entered the rap scene by launching Vibe, *a magazine dedicated to covering hip-hop culture.*

new magazines stepped in to fill the void.

In the summer of 1988 Harvard University student David Mays had a hip-hop show called "Street Beat" on the campus radio station. To promote the show around campus, he created a two-page newsletter entitled *The Source*. He used $250 of his own money to print and copy the newsletter for a mailing list of 1,000 hip-hop music fans. By Mays's senior year *The Source* had a circulation of 10,000. Record retailers caught on and began to distribute it nationwide. After graduation Mays opened an office in New York City, and *The Source* grew to become one of the first magazines dedicated entirely to hip-hop.

Other hip-hop magazines have emerged to compete against the success of *The Source*, including New York–based *XXL* magazine from Harris Publishing; the Los Angeles–based *Rap Pages*, published by *Hustler* founder Larry Flint; as well as the L.A.-based *Stress* and *Rap Sheet* magazines.

In 1993 Quincy Jones teamed up with Time Warner and entered the rap scene with a new magazine dedicated to black culture, called *Vibe*. With its strong, urban-influenced writing and elegant design, *Vibe* hit the streets with the intention of covering the traditionally black music genres that *Rolling Stone* often overlooked. Former *Vibe* president Keith T. Clinkscales told Harvard Business School's Bulletin Online, "*Rolling Stone* created the category of music journalism. We wanted to be *Rolling Stone*, only with different music."

In its six-year history, *Vibe* has seen its circulation grow from 100,000 to 700,000. The oversize monthly has also made successful forays onto the Internet and into the fashion, book publishing, and music industries. However, the magazine was not without its controversies. In 1994 original editor Jonathan Van Meter left *Vibe* in protest after Jones refused his plan to feature Madonna on the cover. Jones felt Madonna was too mainstream and opted to stick to the celebration of black culture. In the following year a cover story on Michael Jackson never discussed the accusations of child molestation that had plagued the star the previous year. Critics viewed the omission as a symbol of the cozy relationship the magazine had with celebrities. In 1996 several black staff members threatened to quit over the appointment of a white editor from *The Source*. In June of 1996, with the magazine's circulation at 400,000, Time Inc. sold its share in *Vibe* to Quincy Jones and his partners.

Unfortunately, the creation of media outlets devoted to hop-hop did not end the conflict between rap and the media. In several high-profile incidents the hip-hop media have provoked the ire of the artists they cover. *The Source*, in particular, has been the target of hip-hop artists who are angry at their portrayal in the magazine. The rap group the Almighty RSO trashed *Source* offices in 1994 after the magazine gave them a bad album review. Also in 1994, *Source* freelancer Cheo Hodari Coker was punched by the Wu-Tang Clan's Master Killa, although he later apologized. That same year, the video for Public Enemy's "I Stand Accused" depicted the group's S1Ws trashing the offices of a rap magazine named *The Sauce*. Cypress Hill has protested against the magazine by burning copies of it during live performances.

The most infamous account of a rapper/journalist face-off occurred with the launch of the *Vibe* magazine spin-off *Blaze*. Unlike *Vibe*, *Blaze* would concentrate solely on hip-hop music and culture. The brainchild of then *Vibe* president Keith T. Clinkscales, *Blaze* debuted with 120 advertising pages. The stories included pieces on Snoop Doggy Dogg, jazz keyboardist and arranger Bob James's contributions to hip-hop, and a "soundclash" competition between two Jamaican mobile audio systems. However, it was editor Jesse Washington's "Manifesto," which announced *Blaze*'s arrival, that increased the demand of the new magazine among hip-hop fans. Washington wrote, "I'm sitting in a conference room at the Hit Factory studios, sunk deep into a leather swivel chair. A nine-millimeter pistol is pointed at my chest. At the trigger end of the gun barrel stands platinum artist Wyclef, tipsy off the vodka. He's heated because *Blaze* is about to give Canibus's new LP, *Can-I-Bus?*, a negative review."

This incident sparked a media feeding frenzy, during which Wyclef denied ever pulling a gun on Washington. The manifesto stated how Wyclef thought it was unfair of *Blaze* to review an unfinished album; *Can-I-Bus?* was not correctly mixed yet. Washington chose not to press charges, partly from mistrust of the police. Wyclef continues to maintain his innocence in the incident. He told MTV that it was a publicity stunt Washington created to sell magazines.

According to the *Guide to New Consumer Magazines, Blaze's* debut, featuring mention of the Wyclef incident in the manifesto, was "the largest music and entertainment magazine launch in publishing history." Yet Washington would suffer for his success. In November of 1998 he was physically attacked by Deric "D-Dot" Angeletti, a record producer who worked with Sean "Puffy" Combs. This time Washington had the cuts and bruises to prove it. According to Washington, Angeletti was upset over the magazine's publishing of a picture that identified him as the Madd Rapper, a fictional character who always spoke passionately of how good rappers like him could never get record deals. The character had made cameos on various albums on the Bad Boy record label, and Angeletti wanted to keep his identity as the Madd Rapper a secret.

Three days after the beating Angeletti and another man voluntarily went to a Manhattan police station for questioning. The two were arrested and charged with felony assault and criminal possession of a weapon, the weapon being a conference-room chair, according to police.

Incidents such as these give the mainstream media more excuses to focus on rap's few performers who seem drawn to violent excess. Luckily, there are signs that some media outlets are beginning to recognize hip-hop's staying power. In February 1999 *Time* magazine featured Lauryn Hill on the cover for its story "Hip-hop Nation." The magazine proclaimed, "There's more to rap than just rhythms and rhymes. After two decades, it has transformed the culture of America."

According to that same article, rap has surpassed country music as the fastest-growing musical category, selling more than 81 million units in 1998—a 31 percent increase over 1997. While rap continues to serve as a mouthpiece for urban America, its acceptance into the mainstream simply underscores its boundless energy and limitless possibilities.

8

Hip-Hop Empires

WHAT STARTED OUT as purely an expression through graffiti, clothing, speech, and rhymes has grown into a multibillion-dollar industry. The goals of kids who yearn to become rap stars have now broadened to include rap producers, label owners, video directors, and A&R (Artists and Repertiore) executives. Several hip-hop artists have successfully parlayed their success on the microphone into business ventures that not only increase their longevity in hip-hop, but also provide opportunities for other young hopefuls to learn the business firsthand.

Russell Simmons spent the 1990s building Def Jam into a multimedia hip-hop enterprise, expanding beyond records and management. By 1991 Def Jam/Rush Associated Labels accounted for roughly 60 percent of the $34 million in revenue from Simmons's company, Rush Communications. By 1992 Rush Communications had become the second-largest black-owned entertainment outfit in the country, behind only Black Entertainment Television. The company was comprised of seven record labels, including Def Jam as well as OBR for Simmons's R&B artists. He had five artist management companies, film and TV production units, and a host of music publishing companies.

Sean "Puffy" Combs, also known as Puff Daddy, poses backstage at the 2000 Grammy Awards. Before becoming a rapper himself, Combs helped manage rappers such as Craig Mack and the Notorious B.I.G. on his record label, Bad Boy Records.

A skit from the half-hour stand-up series Def Comedy Jam, *which first aired in 1992 on HBO. In the '90s Def Jam Records branched off to become a multimedia conglomerate, including an advertising agency and a film division in addition to the TV show.*

In 1992 the television production arm developed the half-hour stand-up series *Def Comedy Jam*, which evolved from Rush's *New Music Report* video show, syndicated by Peter Guber Television. When Peter Guber sold his company to Columbia, Simmons set his sights on finding another format in which to combine hip-hop and comedy. He hooked up with Stan Lathan, director of such TV shows as *Roc* and *Frank's Place*, and together they approached producers Bernie Brillstein and Brad Grey to develop *Def Comedy Jam*. HBO bought the series, and the first episode aired in the winter of 1992.

Ratings for the show soared, prompting HBO to renew it for 22 new episodes.

In September of 1999 Simmons sold his share of Def Jam Records to Universal Music Group. Backstage at the 1999 Source Awards, he said of his transaction, "I've had it for a long time, it's okay to cash something in. I mean, I love what I do, I still do it the same I did it before I sold it, but it's easier for them to gamble it up and down. When we sold the first half of the company, we wanted to give artists a better opportunity. As an independent company it's very difficult [to distribute records]. It's like selling records out of the trunk."

Even though he no longer owns Def Jam, Simmons is far from out of business. He owns the newly created Rush Media, an advertising agency that retains Coca-Cola, Estée Lauder, HBO, and BET as clients. Sales from his clothing line, Phat Fashions, founded in 1993, have skyrocketed from $35 million to more than $100 million. Def Jam Films, which produced Eddie Murphy's 1996 hit *The Nutty Professor,* also produced the sequel, *Nutty Professor II: The Klumps,* which was released in the summer of 2000. A magazine and a television show are in the works as well.

Other promoters would follow in Simmons's successful footsteps. Sean "Puffy" Combs, also called Puff Daddy, went from interning at MCA Records to heading his own multimillion-dollar conglomerate, Bad Boy Entertainment. Born in Harlem in 1970, Sean Combs exhibited an early entrepreneurial spirit by running two paper routes. While attending Howard University in Washington, D.C., Combs convinced his childhood friend Heavy D to get him a job at Uptown Records as an intern. Uptown was headed by Andre Harrell, who in 1981 recorded "Genius Rap" as Dr. Jeckyll of the group Dr. Jeckyll and Mr Hyde. The 19-year-old Combs moved into Harrell's New Jersey home and saw firsthand how to live an extravagant lifestyle. Within two years Harrell made him a vice president of A&R, in charge of signing new talent to the label.

Combs's first success was Jodeci, a four-member group from North Carolina that he fashioned into a harder-edged Boyz II Men. Combs went on to oversee Father MC's 1990 album *Father's Day*, Mary J. Blige's *What's the 411?*, and Heavy D and the Boyz's *Blue Funk*.

The following year Combs was fired from Uptown by its head. Harrell told *Time* magazine that although Combs was "passionate and creative," he had also become "hot tempered." Combs then worked as a remixer, with thoughts of developing his own company, Bad Boy Entertainment. For a year he spent long hours in his apartment with only his employees, until he finally signed two artists, former EPMD roadie Craig Mack and the Notorious B.I.G.

Arista Records president Clive Davis then offered the 23-year-old Combs a three-year distribution deal worth $10 million. The deal required Combs to deliver at least three albums a year. It included incentives and bonuses that would double the original dollar amount. It also allowed him to profit from directing videos and producing artists, on top of the money he already made as the label owner.

Craig Mack's single "Flava in Ya Ear" was the first to be released, in 1994. The song's innovative track stood head and shoulders above anything else on the radio. Its subsequent remix, featuring LL Cool J, Busta Rhymes, Rampage, and the Notorious B.I.G., cracked Billboard's Top 10 and became the first platinum record for Bad Boy.

Next up to bat was B.I.G.'s album *Ready to Die*. The first single, "Big Poppa," reached number six on the pop charts and eventually won Puffy his second platinum single. *Ready to Die* went double platinum, while Mack's album, *Project: Funk Da World*, was certified gold.

In 1995 and 1996 Puffy introduced R&B acts Faith Evans (B.I.G.'s wife), Total, and 112, while continuing to produce hits for several of the industry's hottest R&B acts, including Mariah Carey, Aretha Franklin, Boyz II Men, TLC, and SWV. By the time Combs signed Mase and the Lox in 1996, his Bad Boy label had become a bitter rival to the Death Row empire Suge Knight was building with Dr. Dre on the West Coast.

That rivalry was at its peak when first Death Row's Tupac Shakur and then Bad Boy's the Notorious B.I.G. were gunned down by unknown assailants. The two tragedies resonated throughout all circles of rap. Puffy was grief stricken at the loss of his friend the Notorious B.I.G. and the senselessness that led to the murder. He quit the rap scene for several months. In 1997 he returned with the single "Can't Nobody Hold Me Down," off his debut album, *No Way Out*. The single stayed at number one for almost two months. The second single was an ode to B.I.G. called "I'll Be Missing You," featuring his widow, Faith. Those two singles helped *No Way Out* sell more than a million copies. The record also picked up a Grammy along the way for Best Rap Album.

Puffy has branched out into other business ventures. He publishes *Notorious*, a 150,000-circulation magazine targeted toward the upper-class urban crowd. Puffy is also planning to open the third of his upscale Caribbean-cuisine restaurants in Chicago. He has also planned a line of frozen food, condiments, and juices. He recently launched a clothing line called Sean John and hired a former Ralph Lauren marketing executive to run it. The jeans, jackets, collared shirts, and T-shirts will be sold in Macy's, Bloomingdale's, and specialty stores like Fred Segal. Puffy will use his own Bad Boy videos, concerts, and personal appearances to promote the line. He's also looking to expand into film with the founding of a TV and film production arm.

"Kids don't want to be like Mike anymore," Puffy told *Time* in February of 1999. "Their heroes are rappers. In five years if Master P and I endorse a presidential candidate, we could turn an election. Hip-hop is that deep."

Master P's empire is so vast and lucrative, he could very well be a successful presidential candidate. Born Percy Miller in New Orleans, P has gained legions of die-hard fans. They not only dig the music, tailor-made for Southern tastes, but they also respect P for the way he rose from his humble beginnings to rule his multimillion-dollar empire, called No Limit. His background, which included growing up in the projects, puts him in the same boat as the majority of his fans. In February 1999 Master P told *Time*, "I see myself as a resource for kids. They can say, 'Master P has been through a lot, but he changed his life, and look at him. I can do the same thing.' I think anyone who's a success is an inspiration."

The eldest of five children in his parents' Calliope apartment complex, P spent most of his youth on the basketball court. After his parents divorced when he was 11, he moved with his mother to Richmond, California, located just north of Oakland. After graduating from high school, he attended the University of Houston, where he would eventually earn a basketball scholarship. However, Percy's thoughts gravitated toward business, not basketball. In 1989, using a $10,000 inheritance from his grandfather, Percy opened a record store in Richmond called No Limit.

It took a couple of years for P to turn the business into a record label. In 1991 he released his debut album, *The Ghetto Is Trying to Kill Me*. The album sold big in the San Francisco Bay Area, as well as in his hometown of New Orleans; however, hip-hop critics virtually ignored the album, writing it off as regional fare that would never be accepted beyond Bay Area borders or the South.

Master P began to stock his records with the popular gangsta-type, West Coast beats that sold well in the South. As more records sold and more money began rolling in, P reached out to his relatives and friends to become rappers, producers, and employees of what is now known as the No Limit family.

Soon P would launch No Limit Filmworks, based in Hollywood. Under this banner P would produce film and television projects, such as his development deal with MTV for his show *Juvenile Detention*, a program centering on a military-style boot camp for youth offenders. The Filmworks arm is also launching a bevy of other enterprises, including No Limit's first software product, a futuristic, intergalactic war game pitting No Limit soldiers against killer robots. There is also No Limit Toys, a plan to produce mountain bikes. In May 2000 Master P announced No Limit Communications, which would offer long-distance calling cards, telephone and paging services, and Internet access.

Rapper and No Limit label owner Master P at a news conference. Like Def Jam and Bad Boy Records, No Limit has expanded beyond the world of music with ventures in clothing, communications, and sports management.

One of Master P's more high-profile ventures is No Limit's sports management arm, No Limit Sports. Master P's clients have included New Orleans Saints running back Ricky Williams (who left No Limit Sports in 2000), Oakland Raider cornerback Charles Woodson, and NBA stars Ron Mercer and Dereck Anderson. Run by chief operating officer Tevester Scott, No Limit Sports not only seeks to represent its clients in business deals, but attempts to counsel these young athletes in all of their financial arrangements and investments. According to Scott, the company takes seriously the

Jermaine Dupri, record producer and head of the So So Def conglomerate. Dupri has signed several big R&B and hip-hop artists, including Xscape, Da Brat, Mariah Carey, and TLC.

job of making sure that the clients know how to invest their money properly so that they don't find themselves penniless in the future.

Most of No Limit's clients are young, with an average age of 21 years. The majority come from low-income urban areas and suddenly find themselves swimming in millions of dollars, with no fundamental knowledge of how to manage their newly earned wealth. Scott says the company's background in hip-hop serves as a comfort zone among new clients, who more than likely come from a background where hip-hop figured prominently.

One of No Limit Sports' strengths is that it can offer its clients access to Master P's other entertainment businesses. P tries to instill a business mentality in all of his artists, producers, and athletes. P also skillfully cross-promotes his products by filling each music release with promotional materials for future No Limit releases. The phenomenal success of his No Limit empire has catapulted Master P, with a net worth of $361 million, onto *Forbes* magazine's 2000 list of the 40 richest people under age 40. And he has not yet given up his basketball dream, either: he has continued to pursue a professional hoops career, earning stints with the NBA's Charlotte Hornets and Toronto Raptors in 1999–2000.

Another Southern company that generates multimillions per year is the Atlanta-based So So Def conglomerate, headed by former break-dancer Jermaine Dupri. Born in Atlanta in 1973, Dupri was influenced musically as a youngster by his father, manager Michael Mauldin. Mauldin had coordinated a Diana Ross show in 1982, and Dupri managed to get onstage and dance along with Ross. Soon he began dancing for Herbie Hancock and Cameo before hitting the hip-hop scene as a background dancer for the New York Fresh Festival, featuring Run-DMC, Whodini, and Grandmaster Flash.

At the age of 14, Dupri produced a record and secured a contract for the trio Silk Tymes Leather. Only four years after producing his first act, Jermaine Dupri secured a label deal for his newly formed So So Def record label in Atlanta and quickly began looking for talent. After spotting 12- and 13-year-old Chris Smith and Chris Kelly at a local mall, Dupri was immediately impressed with their look, without so much as a word with the two. Dupri asked them if they could rap. Both said that they could, and Dupri made them his first official So So Def act, named Kris Kross. Their debut album, *Totally Krossed Out*, spent two weeks at number one and quickly sold 4 million copies.

Beginning with the success of Kris Kross, producer-rapper Dupri was consistently able to churn

Actor and rapper Will Smith began his career as part of the duo DJ Jazzy Jeff and the Fresh Prince, then starred in the long-running sitcom, The Fresh Prince of Bel-Air. *He has also starred in hit films such as* Independence Day, Men in Black, *and* Wild Wild West.

out hit after hit for artists signed to his label, such as Xscape and Da Brat, as well as established entertainers like Mariah Carey and TLC.

Dupri continued producing tracks on TLC's first two albums, which sold more than 15 million copies combined. During 1993 and 1994 Dupri debuted two of his new So So Def acts, Xscape and Da Brat. Both debut albums went platinum, thanks in large part to Dupri, and by the end of 1994 he had become one of the most respected R&B producers in the business.

Looking toward the company's future, Jermaine Dupri wants So So Def to become a giant multimedia force in urban music. He plans on incorporating publishing and video production, soundtracks, movies, and television into the company's daily functions.

The rapper who would surpass all of these enterprising young hip-hop moguls in revenues has earned the bulk of his keep in the film and television industry. Will Smith, formerly known as the latter of the duo DJ Jazzy Jeff and the Fresh Prince, has become one of the biggest superstars of his generation. Smith was able to turn his rapping career into a successful television career, which in turn spawned a string of box-office hits.

In 1987 Jazzy Jeff and the Fresh Prince debuted with the record *Rock the House*, which featured the hit single "Girls Ain't Nothing but Trouble." With the success of their 1988 single "Parents Just Don't Understand" they crossed over into the mainstream. The two relied on a nonthreatening, clean-cut, pop-flavored approach in order to stand out among the dominant hard-edged sound of the period.

The group's success led the National Academy of Recording Arts and Sciences (NARAS) to award

DJ Jazzy Jeff and the Fresh Prince the first ever Best Rap Performance Grammy in 1988 for "Parents Just Don't Understand." The pair would go on to win a Grammy in 1991 for Best Rap Performance by a Duo or Group for their single "Summertime." By this time Smith's broad appeal had led to a starring role in the NBC sitcom *The Fresh Prince of Bel-Air*. The show became a steady ratings winner, and suddenly Will Smith was a household name.

He made his feature-film debut in the drama *Where the Day Takes You* in 1993. His next film, *Six Degrees of Separation*, would win him critical acclaim. After starring in the popular action film *Bad Boys* with Martin Lawrence in 1995, Smith carried a succession of megahits, including 1996's *Independence Day*, *Men in Black* the following year, and 1999's *Wild Wild West*.

After the unsolved shooting deaths of Tupac Shakur and the Notorious B.I.G. shook hip-hop to its core, Will Smith finally decided to record his first solo album, *Big Willie Style*, with the intention of bringing positive lyrics back to rap. While accepting a 1999 MTV Video Music Award, Smith proudly celebrated the violence-free nature of his lyrics in his acceptance speech. His success, in spite of the cynical frowns of hard-core hip-hop fans, proves that hip-hop has the ability to make a mogul out of any rapper with the right amount of talent, ambition, and desire.

9

Mainstream Impact

WITH THE GROWING economic strength of the black rapper's voice, the focus of late 20th-century values began to shift from the certainty that the future would finally turn the great-great-grandchildren of slaves into "model" citizens. Jefferson Morley provocatively notes in *Rap Music as American History* that perhaps what might occur instead is "in America blacks and whites alike will celebrate black values, instead of expecting blacks to accept white values." Perhaps that is already taking place. As rap continues to grow as an economic force, it is having an expanding influence on mainstream culture and style.

Some industry analysts estimate urban clothing lines are generating $750 million to $1 billion annually. The numbers can be attributed to hip-hop's long-standing tradition of rappers shouting out the names of the designers they love to wear. Designers who are lucky enough to catch on can sit back and watch their clothing sell itself within hip-hop circles.

Rapper Grand Puba of Brand Nubian was one of the first MCs to mention designer Tommy Hilfiger on a frequent basis. Eventually, it seemed as though a rhyme wasn't legit unless Hilfiger was mentioned at least once.

Many urban clothing lines such as Tommy Hilfiger have become synonymous with hip-hop. Rap stars like Treach (pictured) of Naughty by Nature have served as models for hip-hop gear.

The Tommy Hilfiger corporation designs and markets men's and women's sportswear and jeans, as well as children's clothing. To take full advantage of rap's early acceptance of his clothing, Hilfiger has lavished free gear on many rap stars in hopes they will don the outfits in videos and live appearances. Hilfiger has made it clear that hip-hop is a vital part of his unabashed attempt to target the urban youth market.

Hilfiger's moment of triumph came when Snoop Doggy Dogg performed on *Saturday Night Live* in 1994 dressed from head to toe in Tommy gear. Hilfiger sales increased by $90 million that year. The September 1996 issue of *Rolling Stone* featured the rap group the Fugees with the men prominently sporting clothing with the Tommy Hilfiger logo. In February of 1996 Hilfiger even used a pair of rap stars as runway models: Method Man of the Wu-Tang Clan and Treach of Naughty by Nature.

Independent companies who design clothes strictly for the hip-hop generation—such as FUBU, Karl Kani, and Dada—have suddenly gone from peddling their wares through independent stores in the inner city to having their lines stocked in the biggest department store chains nationwide.

FUBU founder and CEO Daymond John estimates that 40 percent of his expected $200 million in sales this year will come from large department stores instead of the small mom-and-pop urban shops. FUBU, which stands for "For Us, By Us," is one of the biggest-selling outfitters of hip-hop gear. John started the company in 1992 as a means to make and sell his own hats. He turned half of his house into a factory and began churning out hats as well as other clothing. Once John tapped a neighborhood friend, LL Cool J, to endorse the new line, FUBU took off. Cool J wore the hats everywhere—on his newly released book's cover, in videos, and even in his Gap commercial.

Throughout his career, LL Cool J has set hip-hop trends with his clothes and his trademark hats. Here, he sports a shirt by FUBU, which has become one of the biggest-selling lines of hip-hop gear.

FUBU has relied heavily on similar artist endorsements to generate demand for the product. Artists such as Mariah Carey, Mary J. Blige, Boyz II Men, the Fugees, and Snoop Doggy Dogg have also worn their products, as well as such athletes as NBA star Tim Hardaway, the NFL's Simeon Rice, and boxer Mike Tyson.

Timberland boots have been in existence since the early 1950s; however, their popularity in hip-hop increased once fashions began to move toward the rugged, outdoor style of flannels, vests, and quilted jackets during the mid-1990s. It was during this fashion era that Timberlands, or "Timbos," were heavily mentioned in rap records. The waterproof boot even prompted producer Tim "Timbaland" Mosley to adopt the brand as his stage name. Unlike Hilfiger, who actively catered to the urban youth market once he saw his line embraced by hip-hop, Timberland has done very little to acknowledge the heavy support it receives among urban youth.

In 1989 Timberland donated 50 pairs of work boots to City Year, an urban youth service corps. In 1992 the company became a founding national sponsor of City Year, making the first $1 million investment. However, their unwillingness to reach out to rappers interested in cross-promoting with Hilfiger or FUBU leads some critics to believe that mainstream companies are reluctant to do business with hip-hop. In a 1994 interview Timberland's vice president of marketing, Ken Freitas, acknowledged that the company had found itself in the middle of a fashion trend that boosted sales, but the sales increases weren't the result of any shift in marketing strategy.

Eddie Bauer also saw a boost in sales when their outdoor wear hit the hip-hop scene. The company's hooded down-filled parkas, quilted goose-down vests, and exclusively designed brushed flannel shirts were flying off the racks in the early 1990s. Sales were especially high in their urban stores.

As hip-hop moved into the late 1990s, rappers grew tired of the preppy Hilfiger and Eddie Bauer look and began stuffing their lyrics with mentions of high-end designer labels such as DKNY, Versace, and Dolce & Gabbana. In fact, upscale fashion designer Donna Karan incorporated hip-hop's newest fashion trend of high-tech fabrics and styles resembling those worn by scientists into a new line called DKNY Tech. This lower-priced line of clothing acknowledges the trendsetting power of urban teens.

For Tommy Hilfiger, Timberland, DKNY, and all of the other labels embraced by hip-hop, the result is free advertising. On the surface it would seem as though Hilfiger and others were courting a market unable to afford such designer clothes. The majority of true hip-hoppers live in inner cities, which have traditionally been markets overlooked by expensive clothing companies. So why are companies pitching products to the hip-hop crowd? Because for most of the 1990s hordes of suburban kids, both black and white, have followed inner-city idols in adopting everything from music to clothing to language. This crossover appeal can be credited to a reduced division between black and white tastes, via music videos and the Internet. Before the Internet and rap shows on television, it would take decidedly longer for kids to pick up a certain style. Now kids need look no further than a rap video of their favorite artist to learn how low their pants should hang in order for them to be in style. Scoring with inner-city youths can make a product in demand with the larger and more affluent suburban market.

This concept has prospered not only in the world of fashion, but also in other areas of the mainstream, such as advertising. One product that recast its ads to rely heavily on hip-hop themes is Sprite. The soda company's "Five Deadly Women" ad campaign featured five of the hottest female rappers engaged in a martial arts showdown to save hip-hop. Eve, Mia X, Amil, New York radio DJ Angie Martinez, and Roxanne Shante represented a diverse cross section of MCs designed to appeal to every subdemographic in hip-hop.

A previous Sprite ad campaign applied the same cross-promotional tactic. In the wake of the 1998 conflict between East and West Coast rappers that resulted in the shooting death of Tupac Shakur and the Notorious B.I.G., Sprite thought it important to feature rappers from every region of the United States who must eventually unite in order to defeat Voltron, Defender of the Universe. The ad featured Common from Chicago, Fat Joe of New York, Mack

10 of Los Angeles, the Goodie Mob from Atlanta, and, representing the old school, Afrika Bambaataa along with Jazzy Jay. According to Pina Sciarra, the Sprite brand manager at the time, that particular rap ad campaign quadrupled the number of people who say that Sprite is their favorite soda.

For a series of NBA commercials Sprite's parent company, Coca-Cola, hired two of hip-hop's legendary MCs, KRS-One and MC Shan. Even better, they had them face off in a boxing ring, throwing freestyle rhymes instead of punches. The spot was roundly acclaimed, both inside and outside the rap world.

Hip-hop's wholesome rappers have been able to cross over into other unlikely areas of the mainstream. During Kid 'N Play's reign in hip-hop, the group had their own NBC Saturday-morning program, an animated show with live-action segments, produced by Saban Entertainment. The duo also had a line of Kid 'N Play dolls, action figures, and other toys from Mattel. They also lent their marketability to Sprite, starring in a national TV spot at the height of their career.

As hip-hop enters the new millennium, plans are in motion to build a Hip-hop Hall of Fame in Mount Vernon, New York. The city of 67,000 just north of the Bronx is using a $500,000 federal grant to start the process. Mayor Ernest Davis envisions exhibits of memorabilia from such rappers as LL Cool J, Heavy D, and Doug E. Fresh that will educate viewers on the relationship between hip-hop culture and African history.

Perhaps the mix of music, fashion, and sports personalities present at the 1999 Source Music Awards sums up the lasting impact that hip-hop has made on mainstream America. According to *Los Angeles Times* fashion writer Booth Moore, "the mix of clothes was the ordinary with the extraordinary: designer furs and leather with athletic team jerseys,

Nike sneakers, diamond bracelets, and mall brands like Guess and FUBU. It is the amalgamation of music." Moore wrote, "These real people—albeit very rich real people—have grabbed the fashion world by the horns and made it their own."

Many of the artists and entrepreneurs were sporting outfits from their own clothing line, including rapper Busta Rhymes, Los Angeles Lakers center Shaquille O'Neal, and FUBU owner Daymond John. Rappers, athletes, R&B stars, and designers all came together in celebration of hip-hop, an art form born of the parks in the Bronx as an expression of black inner-city youth.

Rap is not just about making money and setting trends in clothing. It is a documentary of an entire youth culture growing and expressing itself over 21 exciting years. Its strength lies in its mass appeal and its power as a vehicle for urban self-expression. It can also be a powerful force for good.

Five-time Grammy winner Lauryn Hill sees herself as a model for the dispossessed, guiding the development of a positive identity for the young and the poor. To do just that, she founded a non-profit organization, the Refugee Project, in 1996. According to a press release for one of its benefits, the Refugee Project "hopes to create a powerful and supportive network throughout the African diaspora that will give young people the experience and encouragement that is too often missing from their lives." Significantly, Lauryn Hill is joined in her project by many of the big male names in rap, such as Busta Rhymes, Wyclef Jean, and Sean "Puffy" Combs.

Rap in its maturity is reaching higher and deeper, as Hilary Rosen, president and CEO of the Recording Industry Association of America, stated to the Senate Committee on Governmental Affairs in 1998. She called attention to the leadership role rappers, like African griots, can take. She said, "You

Lauryn Hill, along with many other hip-hop artists, have used their influence and resources to give back to their communities. In 1996 Hill founded the Refugee Project, a nonprofit organization helping the young and the poor.

see this in Heavy D's involvement in Operation Unity, promoting racial harmony in America's cities . . . Ice Cube's non-profit Brotherhood Crusade to aid the homeless and the elderly . . . Queen Latifah's Daddy's House, providing educational opportunities for underprivileged children."

Rosen told a reporter in 1999, "Rap and hip-hop artists in America have a unique ability to connect with young people. They take this connection very seriously and use their success to enhance the lives of young adults. These artists impress me every day with their heartfelt contributions that profoundly impact scores of people and communities across the country."

Each rapper is now a thread in the whole, rather than one performer bearing the burden of the entire community. In the 21st century there will be a need for many griots. The most pressing issue facing young people in the new millennium may not be whether rap music has a lasting future, but rather which rappers to follow: the griots of war or the griots of peace? One thing is certain, however: whichever choice young people make, rap will be a cultural and economic force in America for years to come.

CHRONOLOGY

1977   The disastrous impact of the Cross-Bronx Expressway, implemented by legendary city planner Robert Moses, sparks reactions that would begin the birth of hip-hop culture.

1979   Sugar Hill Records releases "Rapper's Delight," which becomes a huge hit and the renowned classic of rap music.

1982   Grandmaster Flash and the Furious Five's critically acclaimed song "The Message" becomes the biggest rap hit to date.

1984   College student Russell Simmons cofounds Def Jam Records with Rick Rubin.

1984   Run-DMC becomes the hottest rap group in the country with the hit "It's Like That."

1986   The Beastie Boys become the first white rap group to go to the top of the charts with the album *Licensed to Ill*.

1988   David Mays and Jon Shecter, students at Harvard University, start the first hip-hop publication, *The Source*, from their college dorm.

1989   N.W.A. bring gangsta rap out of the shadows with their best-selling *Straight Outta Compton*. It brings Los Angeles gang lifestyle to national attention.

1990   The 2 Live Crew gains national attention in several court battles that test freedom of speech laws.

1990   Will Smith transforms his comedic party-rap recording career into an acting career, starring in the sitcom *The Fresh Prince of Bel-Air*.

1991   The film industry picks up on the hip-hop movement with *New Jack City*, starring Ice-T; other films, such as *Boyz N the Hood* and *Menace II Society*, carry the new urban message to another genre.

1992   President Clinton makes rap activist Sister Souljah's message a campaign issue as he attacks her controversial views on race.

1993   Snoop Doggy Dogg releases his album *Doggystyle*, which immediately rushes to the top of the charts.

1996   The Fugees mix the reggae beat with a creative lyrical attitude that gets global attention. Rapper-actor Tupac Shakur dies in a drive-by shooting.

1997   The Notorious B.I.G. is shot and killed in Los Angeles. His album *Life After Death* becomes a huge hit.

1998   Actor Warren Beatty assumes a rap persona to criticize politics in his film *Bulworth*.

1999   Lauryn Hill receives ten Grammy nominations and wins five awards.

SOME CLASSIC RAP ALBUMS

Planet Rock
      1982, Afrika Bambaataa

The Message
      1982, Grandmaster Flash and the Furious Five

Licensed to Ill
      1986, The Beastie Boys

Raising Hell
      1986, Run-DMC

Criminal Minded
      1987, Boogie Down Productions

It Takes a Nation of Millions to Hold Us Back
      1988, Public Enemy

Straight Outta Compton
      1989, N.W.A.

Mama Said Knock You Out
      1990, LL Cool J

Death Certificate
      1991, Ice Cube

The Chronic
      1993, Dr. Dre

Enter the Wu-Tang (36 Chambers)
      1993, The Wu-Tang Clan

Clement, Gary O. "The Heartbeat of African-American Music." *Upscale*, June/July 1993, 32–36.

Farley, Christopher John. "Hip-hop Nation." *Time* 8 February 1999, 54–59.

Fernando, S. H., Jr. *The New Beats*. New York: Anchor Books, 1994.

Greene, Meg. *Lauryn Hill*. Philadelphia: Chelsea House, 2000.

Hale, Thomas A. *Griots and Griottes: Masters of Words and Music*. Bloomington, Ind.: Indiana University Press, 1998.

Jones, Maurice K. *Say It Loud: The Story of Rap Music*. Brookfield, Conn.: Millbrook Press, 1994.

Rose, Tricia. *Black Noise: Rap Music and Black Culture in Contemporary America*. Middletown, Conn.: Wesleyan University Press, 1994.

Saunders, Cherie. "The Titan." *Rap Pages*, July 1999, 97–101.

Stancell, Steven. *Rap Whoz Who*. New York: Schirmer Books, 1996.

Stauffer, Stacey. *Will Smith*. Philadelphia: Chelsea House, 1999.

INDEX

INDEX

page

2: © Jeffrey Scales/Corbis
8: London Features International LTD/ Gregg De Guire
11: The New York Public Library
12: Library of Congress
16-17: © UPI/Corbis-Bettmann
21: AP/Wide World Photos
22: © Robert Hepler/The Everett Collection
24: London Features International LTD/ Jhon Wlaschin
27: © Ernie Paniccioli/Corbis
28: Globe Photos, Inc.
30: AP/Wide World Photos
32: London Features International LTD/ Ron Wolfson
37: © Fitzroy Barrett/Globe Photos, Inc.

40-41: © John Bellissimo/Corbis
42: London Features International LTD/ Ron Wolfson
46a: © Dave Hogan/Corbis
46b: The Everett Collection
49: © Andre Grossman/ Corbis
52: AP/Wide World Photos
54: © Joe Giron/Corbis
56: AP/Wide World Photos
58: AP/Wide World Photos
61: AP/Wide World Photos
66: AP/Wide World Photos
68: AP/Wide World Photos
74: Globe Photos, Inc.
76: London Features International LTD/ George Du Bose
78: AP/Wide World Photos
81: © AFP/Corbis

85: AP/Wide World Photos
90: AP/Wide World Photos
92: The Everett Collection
97: AP/Wide World Photos
98: © Ernie Paniccioli/Corbis
100: © Walter Weissman/ Globe Photos, Inc.
102: AP/Wide World Photos
105: © Reuters/Jeff Christensen/Archive Photos
110: London Features International LTD/ Caroline Torem Craig

COOKIE LOMMEL started her career as a journalist in the entertainment industry. She has interviewed hundreds of film, television, and music personalities as an on-camera reporter for CNN. Her other books include biographies of Madame C. J. Walker, Robert Church, and Johnnie L. Cochran Jr.